总主编　童敬东
总顾问　陆松岩

职场
综合英语
实训手册

基础篇
（第二版）

主　编　王文婷
副主编　杨　柳　唐四保
编　者　王　诚　汪江红　郑礼常　秦　勤
　　　　唐　寅　丁　凡　叶　玫　余　璇

Vocational
Comprehensive
English-Training
Course

北京大学出版社
PEKING UNIVERSITY PRESS

图书在版编目(CIP)数据

职场综合英语实训手册. 基础篇/王文婷主编. —2版. —北京：北京大学出版社，2017.9
（全国职业技能英语系列教材）

ISBN 978-7-301-28615-9

Ⅰ.①职… Ⅱ.①王… Ⅲ.①英语—高等职业教育—习题集 Ⅳ.①H319.6

中国版本图书馆CIP数据核字（2017）第199532号

书　　名	职场综合英语实训手册（基础篇）（第二版） ZHICHANG ZONGHE YINGYU SHIXUN SHOUCE（JICHUPIAN）
著作责任者	王义婷　主编
责任编辑	刘文静
标准书号	ISBN 978-7-301-28615-9
出版发行	北京大学出版社
地　　址	北京市海淀区成府路205号　100871
网　　址	http://www.pup.cn　新浪微博：@北京大学出版社
电子信箱	liuwenjing008@163.com
电　　话	邮购部 62752015　发行部 62750672　编辑部 62754382
印 刷 者	北京鑫海金澳胶印有限公司
经 销 者	新华书店
	787毫米×1092毫米　16开本　8.5印张　270千字
	2012年8月第1版
	2017年9月第2版　2019年9月第3次印刷
定　　价	28.00元

未经许可，不得以任何方式复制或抄袭本书之部分或全部内容。
版权所有，侵权必究
举报电话：010-62752024　电子信箱：fd@pup.pku.edu.cn
图书如有印装质量问题，请与出版部联系，电话：010-62756370

第二版前言

《职场综合英语实训手册》是《职场综合英语教程》的配套用书。本书第一版在编写的时候，既照顾了主教材《职场综合英语教程》的单元主题，也参考了英语应用能力考试(B级)的试卷形式，为学习者进一步掌握主教材内容和准备英语应用能力考试提供了必要的资料。然而，第一版面世以来已经过去了五个春秋，高职高专的生源已经悄然发生了变化，英语应用能力考试也于2014年换了新的考试大纲。在此形势下，对原书进行修订，使之与时俱进，更好地服务于高职高专英语教学的需要就成了我们的共识。

在北京大学出版社的大力支持下，原书主编对第一版《职场综合英语教程》及其配套用书从形式到内容进行了研讨，并在此基础上统一了修改意见。《职场综合英语实训手册》的修订工作仍然由各分册主编负责，参加修订的编者还是原班人马。如此分工既能保证本套教材内容的延续性，又能保证其质量的稳定性。在具体的修订中，我们主要做了如下三项工作：

1. 根据《职场综合英语教程》（第二版）的内容，把原书中设定为八个单元的练习进行压缩，改成六个单元的练习；
2. 对原书中的部分阅读理解和英译汉内容进行修订，使之与最新英语应用能力考试(B级)接轨；
3. 以新型英语应用能力考试(B级)真题代替业已淘汰的旧真题。

修订后的《职场综合英语实训手册》难度有所降低，更加适合学习者利用课外时间自学，有利于促进学习者对课堂内容的消化，有助于学习者了解和迎接英语应用能力考试。

当然，尽管我们进行了认真的修订，书中仍然可能会存在这样或那样的谬误，希望大家在使用的过程中发现这些不足，及时反馈给我们，以便我们在下次修订时更正。

编者
2017年7月

第一版前言

《职场综合英语教程》是一套由西方文化入手,渐进涉及职场工作需要的高职英语教材。该教材遵循"以服务为宗旨,以就业为导向"的原则,结合高职英语教学的需要和高职学生的实际英语水平,具有较强的实用性和针对性。《职场综合英语实训手册》(基础篇)(以下简称《实训手册》)是《职场综合英语教程》(基础篇)(以下简称《教程》)的辅助教程,内容上与《教程》(基础篇)有所兼顾,保持了密切的联系。同时又充分考虑到"高等学校英语应用能力考试(B级)"(以下简称"B级考试")的实考题型,在结构上对"B级考试"的题型进行了部分套用。这样设计的目的有三:一、增强学生的动手能力,包括记录所听材料的关键词、写摘要、翻译英语语句、用英语写应用文等。二、通过练习检测学生学习《教程》(基础篇)的效果,帮助教师了解学生学习中的困难,从而更有效地施教。三、帮助学生了解"B级考试"的要求,以便学生顺利通过这项旨在检测高职学生英语是否合格的等级考试。教师可安排学生每学完一个单元的《教程》中的内容就完成一套《实训手册》中的练习,以巩固课堂学习所获得的知识。

《实训手册》(基础篇)包含六个单元的练习,每单元练习由六个部分组成。分别是:Listening Comprehension、Dialogue、Vocabulary & Structure、Reading Comprehension、Translation 和 Writing,并在内容上尽可能保持与《教程》(基础篇)的单元内容一致。在各种题型中,Listening Comprehension 中除了B级考试的三种听力题型,还增加了单词辨音,目的是锻炼学生对各发音相近的音素能进行辨识。Dialogue 部分选取一些日常生活中的场景,如问候、介绍、提供建议帮助等,训练学生的情景应答,以提高他们的语言实践性。Vocabulary & Structure 这部分除了B级考试题型,还增加了选词填空和选择恰当的词进行句子同义改写,目的是帮助学生了解不同词性的不同用法并归纳总结一些常见的词性转换规律,以此扩大学生的词汇量,提高英语学习的能力。同义改写是检查学生对本单元一些重点词汇和短语的学习,帮助他们加深理解。Writing 部分除了练习写一篇和课本对应的应用文外,还增加了连词成句的练习,目的是训练学生遣词造句的能力,熟悉英语基本句型框架,帮助一些基础比较薄弱的学生巩固英语的基础知识,为后续课程的学习奠定必要的基础。

在对《实训手册》(基础篇)进行实际训练时,建议学生把重点放在做题方法上。比如,做"Vocabulary & Structure"的要点是发现题干中的关键词。

例题:

16. The report gives a _____ picture of the company's future development.

  A. central   B. clean   C. clear   D. comfortable

(2010年12月试卷)

做这一题的要点是把题干中的 picture 看作关键词。所给选项中 central 表示"中心的"、clean 表示"清洁的"、clear 表示"清晰的"、comfortable 表示"舒服的"。只有 clear 与 picture 搭配最好;因此,属于最佳选项。

再看一例:

26. Could you tell me the (different) _____ between American and British English in business writing?

(2010年12月试卷)

本题的关键词是空白处前面的 tell。所填词显然应该是 tell 的宾语,different 是形容词,不能做宾语,应填 difference。

我们再以阅读理解为例。下面是 2010 年 12 月"B 级考试"的实考题:

MEMO

To: Katherine Anderson,Manager
From: Stephen Black,Sales Department
Date: 19 November,2010
Subject: Resignation(辞职)

Dear Ms. Katherine Anderson,

  I am writing to inform you of my intention to resign(辞职)from G&S Company.

  I very much appreciate my four years' working for the company. The training has been excellent and I have gained valuable experience working within an efficient and friendly team environment. In particular, I am very grateful for your personal guidance during these first years of my career.

  I feel now that it is time to further develop my knowledge and skills in a different environment.

第一版前言

I would like to leave, if possible, in a month's time on Saturday, 18 December. This will allow me to complete my current job responsibilities. I hope that this suggested arrangement is acceptable to the company.

Once again, thank you for your attention.

Memo

Date: 19 November, 2010
Memo to: Katherine Anderson, (46) _____
Memo from: (47) _____, Sales Department
Subject: Resignation
Years of working for G&S Company: (48) _____
Reasons for leaving: to further develop (49) _____ in another environment
Time of leaving the position: on (50) _____

做类似题目的要点是带着题目在原文中找结构,因此,很多时候不需要对原文进行逐句阅读。

就上述题目而言,(46)的要点在于填空前面的词:Katherine Anderson;(47)的要点是填空后面的词:Sales Department;(48)的要点在于填空前面的词:G&S Company;(49)的要点在于填空前面的词:further develop;(50)的要点在于填空前面的词:Time 和 on。

根据以上线索不难发现,本题的答案是:(46) Manager;(47) Stephen Black;(48) four/4;(49) knowledge and skills;(50) Saturday, 18 December。

《实训手册》(基础篇)由安徽高职外语教研会组织编写。在《实训手册》(基础篇)的编写过程中我们参考了大量的文字资料,对这些有关资料的编者我们深表感谢。同时,我们也深深知道,尽管我们认真地对本教程进行了审阅,书中错误仍然在所难免。在此,我们真诚地希望各位教师和同学在使用本书的过程中把编写之错漏记下来反馈给我们,以便我们以后通过修订,使本书臻于完善。

编者
2012 年 6 月

目 录

Unit 1　Campus Life ··· (1)
 Part Ⅰ　Listening Comprehension ··· (1)
 Part Ⅱ　Dialogue ··· (3)
 Part Ⅲ　Vocabulary & Structure ··· (5)
 Part Ⅳ　Reading Comprehension ··· (9)
 Part Ⅴ　Translation ·· (13)
 Part Ⅵ　Writing ·· (14)

Unit 2　Pop Music ·· (17)
 Part Ⅰ　Listening Comprehension ··· (17)
 Part Ⅱ　Dialogue ··· (19)
 Part Ⅲ　Vocabulary & Structure ··· (22)
 Part Ⅳ　Reading Comprehension ··· (25)
 Part Ⅴ　Translation ·· (29)
 Part Ⅵ　Writing ·· (30)

Unit 3　Sports ·· (32)
 Part Ⅰ　Listening Comprehension ··· (32)
 Part Ⅱ　Dialogue ··· (34)
 Part Ⅲ　Vocabulary & Structure ··· (36)
 Part Ⅳ　Reading Comprehension ··· (40)

Part V	Translation	(45)
Part VI	Writing	(46)

Unit 4　Food Culture (48)

Part Ⅰ	Listening Comprehension	(48)
Part Ⅱ	Dialogue	(50)
Part Ⅲ	Vocabulary & Structure	(52)
Part Ⅳ	Reading Comprehension	(57)
Part Ⅴ	Translation	(61)
Part Ⅵ	Writing	(62)

Unit 5　Movie (64)

Part Ⅰ	Listening Comprehension	(64)
Part Ⅱ	Dialogue	(66)
Part Ⅲ	Vocabulary & Structure	(68)
Part Ⅳ	Reading Comprehension	(72)
Part Ⅴ	Translation	(76)
Part Ⅵ	Writing	(77)

Unit 6　Mother and Child (79)

Part Ⅰ	Listening Comprehension	(79)
Part Ⅱ	Dialogue	(81)
Part Ⅲ	Vocabulary & Structure	(83)
Part Ⅳ	Reading Comprehension	(88)
Part Ⅴ	Translation	(92)
Part Ⅵ	Writing	(93)

答案及听力材料 (95)

Unit 1 Campus Life

Part I Listening Comprehension

Task 1

Directions: *In this section you will hear 10 sentences. You are required to circle the word that you hear in brackets.*

1. The (boat/bought) is very small.
2. I want you to (feel/fill) this dish.
3. The old man's (pan/pen) leaks.
4. I (hope/help) that you will have a good time.
5. Is he going to (leave/live)?
6. This (time/tame) he needs to have a lunch with your family.
7. Please sit (done/down).
8. Li Ming's (hat/hate) is very beautiful.
9. At length the young girl found her (key/king) to the lab.
10. At last, the boy (gates/gets) to the bus station.

Task 2

Directions: *In this section you will hear one word from each of the following groups of words. Circle the one you hear.*

1.	serve	service	surface	search
2.	leaf	belief	life	knife
3.	very	every	various	way
4.	sip	sleep	six	sink
5.	zinc	zip	zap	zebra
6.	ton	down	bun	tongue
7.	card	cart	part	park
8.	late	gate	eight	greet
9.	oil	boil	soil	toy
10.	shave	sheep	ship	shimmer

Task 3

Directions: *This section is to test your ability to give proper responses. There are 5 recorded questions in it. After each question, there is a pause. When you hear a question, you should decide on the correct answer from the 4 choices marked A, B, C and D.*

1. A. Yes, he is my dad.   B. Yes, it is red.
   C. Is he a doctor?   D. My friend likes it.
2. A. I'm fine.   B. Hi, this is my father.
   C. Good morning.   D. How do you do?
3. A. I'm from Shanghai.   B. Beijing is a big city.
   C. I am a student.   D. Are you from Anhui?
4. A. Today is Sunday.   B. Yes. It's eight thirty.
   C. No, I think so.   D. It's fine.
5. A. Yes, they are.   B. Today is fine.
   C. No one like it.   D. Ok. Let's begin.

Task 4

Directions: *This section is to test your ability to understand short dialogues. There are 5 recorded dialogues in it. After each dialogue, there is a recorded question. When you hear a question, you should decide on the correct*

Unit 1 Campus Life

answer from the 4 choices marked A, B, C and D.

1. A. About the book.   B. The date.
   C. The time.   D. About cooking.
2. A. Check in.   B. About England.
   C. Twenty past seven.   D. About internet.
3. A. In the book store.   B. In the drug store.
   C. In the supermarket.   D. In the post office.
4. A. Five dollars.   B. Fifteen dollars.
   C. Ten dollars.   D. Twenty dollars.
5. A. Buying an apple.   B. Buying a bike for his son.
   C. Buying a bike for himself.   D. Talking about color.

Task 5

Directions: *In this section, you will hear a short passage. There are five missing words or phrases in it. Fill in the blanks with the exact words or phrases you hear.*

These are the things we learn. No matter how old you are, share everything. Don't hit people and play (1)_____. Keep your (2)_____ room clean and put things back where you found them. Don't take things that aren't yours. Wash your hands before you eat. When you (3)_____ somebody, you must say you're sorry. Don't make (4)_____ when someone is studying or sleeping. Get into good (5)_____. Get up early and never be late for school or work. Go to bed on time. Always remember to learn.

Part II   Dialogue

Task 1

Directions: *Complete the following conversation by making the best choice in the table below.*

John: Hello! Is that Mike speaking?

Mike: (1)_____

John: Mike, do you like your new school?

Mike: Yes, very much. But things are quite different here.

John: Really? (2)_____

Mike: Yes, I go to school every day. But on Friday afternoon we must join the school clubs.

John: Sounds great! (3)_____

Mike: Seven subjects. They are English, math, history, science, physics, art and P. E.

John: (4)_____

Mike: I like math best. My math teacher says I am doing well in it.

John: (5)_____

A: Yes, this is Mike speaking.

B: Well done!

C: Do you go to school every day?

D: What is your favorite subject?

E: That's too bad.

F: Yes, I am.

G: How many subjects do you have?

Task 2

Directions: *The following are some ways of greeting and bidding farewell. Read the words spoken and then match them with the functions.*

Words Spoken

A. I'm afraid I must leave now.

B. Let's have lunch sometime.

C. How are you getting on?

D. How's your mother?

E. Fancy meeting you here!

Unit 1 Campus Life

F. Couldn't be better.

G. See you.

H. Hi! How are you doing?

I. It's been a long time since we last met.

Functions

1. Saying you have to leave

2. Saying you hope to see someone again sometime.

3. Saying you're surprised to see someone.

4. Greeting your friend.

5. Asking about someone.

6. Greet someone and emphasize that you haven't seen him/her for a long time.

7. Use a casual way of saying goodbye to someone you know well.

8. Greet someone in passing on your way to work.

9. Respond to someone's greeting by saying that your life is really good.

Part Ⅲ Vocabulary & Structure

Task 1

Directions: *Complete each statement by choosing the appropriate answer from the 4 choices marked A, B, C and D.*

1. When the teacher praised him for working out the maths problem, Jack looked _____ at his classmates.

    A. proud　　　　B. proudly　　　　C. pride　　　　D. pridely

2. To everyone's _____, the girl finished the job quite well.

    A. satisfied　　B. satisfactory　　C. satisfying　　D. satisfaction

3. — What are you doing here?

    — Oh, my teacher asked me to write a passage about _____ in English.

    — You can write _____ passage in English?

    A. 600 words; a 600-words　　　　B. 600-word; a 600-words

C. 600 words; a 600-word   D. 600 words; a 600-words

4. No one should enter the spot without the _____ of the police.

   A. permit   B. permission   C. permitting   D. permittence

5. _____ do you _____ the TV play? — Not bad, I think.

   A. How; think of   B. What; like
   C. How; like   D. What; think

6. I _____ have a good time _____ the party.

   A. hope you will; at   B. like you; on
   C. hope you to; in   D. want you that; from

7. My TV is out of order. Can you tell me what the _____ news about Iraq War is?

   A. lately   B. latest   C. later   D. latter

8. The Great Wall is more than 6,000 li in _____.

   A. longer   B. longing   C. long   D. length

9. To my _____, I passed the exam easily.

   A. joy   B. joyful   C. joyless   D. joyness

10. Canada is mainly an _____ country.

    A. English-spoken   B. speak-English
    C. English-speaking   D. spoken-English

11. What a pity my new CD player doesn't work! _____ must be something wrong with it.

    A. It   B. There   C. This   D. That

12. Their new neighbor _____ blond hair and blue eyes.

    A. is having   B. have   C. has   D. had

13. Would you please _____ again?

    A. explain it me   B. explain me it
    C. explain it to me   D. explain to me it

14. There _____ a heavy rain this evening.

    A. will have   B. has   C. will be   D. have

15. _____ noisy children! Go and ask them to keep quiet.

    A. What   B. What a   C. How   D. How a

Unit 1 Campus Life

Task 2

Directions: *There are 10 incomplete statements here. You should fill each blank with the proper form of the word given in brackets.*

1. More than 30 firms _____ in the project. (involve)

2. In four-star hotels, breakfast _____ in the bill. (include)

3. Candidates should have training and _____ experience in basic electronics. (practice)

4. The law requires equal treatment for all, _____ of race, religion, or sex. (regard)

5. Your introduction should _____ your skills and achievements. (highlight)

6. Britain wants _____ its position as a world power. (maintain)

7. They're encouraged to think _____ about themselves and their future. (positive)

8. All the rooms have _____ views. (splendid)

9. It was a wonderful film, but not a _____ success. (finance)

10. The _____ of the students have signed up for this activity. (major)

Task 3

Directions: *Pay attention to different parts of speech and select the appropriate word to fill in the blanks.*

a. confident, confidence, confidently

1. He had complete _____ in the doctors.

2. We have to do what is right _____.

3. He is quietly _____ that there will be no problems this time.

b. add, addition, additional

1. The soup is too salty, please _____ some sugar to it.

2. If you need some _____ information, you can visit our website.

3. In _____ to swimming, he also likes dancing and drawing.

c. practice, practical, impractical

1. Anybody who wants to master a skill should remember that _____ makes perfect.

2. The manager shook his head to my plan because he thought it _____.

3. It is hoped that all college students pass _____ English tests.

d. recommend, recommendation, recommended

1. Doctors strongly _____ that fathers should be present at their baby's birth.

2. The best way of finding a lawyer is through personal _____.

3. Though ten years old, this book is highly _____.

e. adequate, inadequate, adequately

1. Many students are not _____ prepared for higher education.

2. One in four people worldwide are without _____ homes.

3. The teacher made us feel _____ if we made mistakes.

Task 4

Directions: *Rewrite the following sentences with the expressions in the box.*

| regardless of | adapt to | precious | tempt |
| be aware of | take in | start with | highlight |

1. The salesman finds it easy to cheat old ladies.

   _____

2. I went out in spite of the rain.

   _____

3. If you were in the Sahara, you would realize the value of fresh water.

   _____

4. Nothing would attract me to live here.

___

5. The English alphabet begins with A.

___

6. His remarks stressed his own function.

___

7. Her family's support is particularly important to Mary.

___

8. Her eyes took a while to accommodate to the darkness.

___

Part IV   Reading Comprehension

Task 1

Directions: *Read the following passage and make the correct choice.*

As any homemaker who has tried to keep order at the dinner table knows, there is far more to a family meal than food. Sociologist Michael Lewis has been studying 50 families to find out just how much more.

Lewis and his co-workers carried out their study by videotaping (录像) the families while they ate ordinary meals in their own homes. They found that parents with small families talk actively with each other and their children. But as the number of children gets larger, conversation gives way to the parents' efforts to control the loud noise they make. That can have an important effect on the children. "In general, the more question-asking the parents do, the higher the children's IQ scores," Lewis says. "And the more children there are, the less question-asking there is."

The study also provides an explanation for why middle children often seem to have a harder time in life than their siblings (兄弟姐妹). Lewis found that in families with three or four children, dinner conversation is likely to center on the oldest child, who has the most to talk about, and the youngest, who needs the most attention. "Middle children are invisible," says Lewis. "When you see someone get up from the table and walk around during dinner, chances are the middle child." There is, however, one thing that stops all conversation and prevents anyone from having attention: "When the TV is on," Lewis says, "dinner is a non-event."

1. The writer's purpose in writing the text is to _____.

   A. show the relationship between parents and children

   B. teach parents ways to keep order at the dinner table

   C. report on the findings of a study

   D. give information about family problems

2. Parents with large families ask fewer questions at dinner because _____.

   A. they are busy serving food to their children

   B. they are busy keeping order at the dinner table

   C. they have to pay more attention to younger children

   D. they are tired out having prepared food for the whole family

3. By saying "Middle children are invisible" in paragraph 3, Lewis means that middle children _____.

   A. have to help their parents to serve dinner

   B. get the least attention from the family

   C. are often kept away from the dinner table

   D. find it hard to keep up with other children

4. Lewis' research provides an answer to the question _____.

   A. why TV is important in family life

   B. why parents should keep good order

   C. why children in small families seen to be quieter

   D. why middle children seem to have more difficulties in life

5. Which of the following statements would the writer agree to?

   A. It is important to have the right food for children.

   B. It is a good idea to have the TV on during dinner.

   C. Parents should talk to each of their children frequently.

   D. Elder children should help the younger ones at dinner.

Unit 1 Campus Life

Task 2

Directions: *The following is a list of terms frequently used in a school. After reading it, you are required to find the items equivalent to（与……等同）those given in Chinese in the table below.*

A — President's Office
B — Postgraduate Certificates
C — alumni meeting
D — selective/optional course
E — open-book exam
F — associate diploma
G — technical school
H — Administration Office
I — Students' Club
J — canteen
K — student hostel
L — lecture theatre
M — teaching facilities
N — open an account
O — opening ceremony
P — voluntary labour
Q — campus job fairs

Example：技校(G)　　　　　　学生俱乐部(I)
1. 选修课(　　)　　　　　　开卷考试(　　)
2. 学生公寓(　　)　　　　　阶梯教室(　　)
3. 开学典礼(　　)　　　　　食堂(　　)
4. 义务劳动(　　)　　　　　校园招聘会(　　)
5. 校长办公室(　　)　　　　教学设施(　　)

Task 3

Directions: *Complete the information by filling in the blanks. Write your answers in no more than 3 words.*

Over a million people visit Hawaii each year because of its beautiful weather and wonderful scenery. The Hawaiian Islands have very mild temperatures. For example, August, the hottest month, averages 78.4°F, while February, the coldest month, averages 71.9°F. In addition, the rainfall in Hawaii is not very heavy because mountains on the north of each island stop incoming storms. For instance, Honolulu averages only 23 inches of rain per year. This beautiful weather helps tourists to enjoy Hawaii's wonderful natural scenery, from mountain waterfalls to fields of flowers and fruits. And Hawaii's beautiful beaches are everywhere — from the lovely Kona coast beaches on the large island of Hawaii to Waikiki Beach on Oahu. Warm sunshine and beautiful beaches — it is not surprising that so many people visit Hawaii each year. Are you going to join us? Don't miss the chance!

> Hawaii
> Famous for its (1) _____ and (2) _____
> Average Temperature: ranging from (3) _____ to 78.4°F
> Annual rainfall in Honolulu: (4) _____
> Attractions for tourists: (5) _____ and beautiful beaches

Task 4

***Directions**: Complete the answers in no more than 3 words.*

Hello, ladies and gentlemen, welcome to Beijing. Below is the schedule of your trip this morning:

7:00 a.m. Breakfast in the hotel

8:00 a.m. Leave for the Tian'anmen Square

9:30 a.m. Leave for the Temple of Heaven

11:00 a.m. Leave for the hotel

After the tour we will be returning for lunch in the hotel. Lunch will be in the ballroom. This afternoon at 2 p.m. buses leave for the Summer Palace. They then continue onto the Friendship Store for shopping at 3:45 p.m.. There is then a short walk to dinner at the windows on the World Restaurant. Dress is very casual in the restaurant, no jackets or ties required for the men.

1. Who do you think may announce the schedule?

   A guide or a person who is working in _____.

Unit 1 Campus Life

2. What is the time for breakfast in the hotel?

   At _____.

3. Where will the tourists go at 9:30 a.m.?

   They will leave the Tian'anmen Square for the _____.

4. When will the tourists be arranged to go shopping?

   At _____.

5. How can the men be dressed in the restaurant?

   Very casual, no _____ required.

Part Ⅴ Translation

Directions: *This part is to test your ability to translate English into Chinese. Make the best choice.*

1. It may be convenient for you to eat out, but it can end up costing you a lot of money.

   A. 出去吃饭是方便,但你最终要花掉很多钱的。

   B. 你可能出去吃饭,结束时要花掉很多钱。

   C. 也许你出去吃饭,但你花很多钱。

2. College life is very free and exciting, but we also have a great responsibility.

   A. 大学生活是免费又刺激的,但是我们有许多责任。

   B. 大学生活虽然是义务的,激动人心的,但我们也肩负着许多的责任。

   C. 大学生活虽然很自由,很精彩,但我们也肩负着重大的责任。

3. College life has given us a new experience —an independent way of life.

   A. 大学生活给了我一个新的经验——单独的生活方式。

   B. 大学生活让我们获得了新的经验——独自生活的经验。

   C. 大学生活给我们一种全新的体验——独立自主的生活方式。

4. Although I no longer have summer holidays from school, I still feel sad to see summer behind me.

   A. 虽然我不再有暑假了,但夏天要结束的时候我仍然感到难过。

   B. 虽然学校不再放暑假了,但夏天要结束的时候我仍然感到难过。

   C. 虽然我不再有暑假了,看到夏天在我背后我仍然感到难过。

5. You want to succeed in whatever you do.

   A. 你想成功,无论你做什么。

   B. 无论你做什么,你都想成功。

   C. 你想成功做好任何事。

6. Chinese people and westerners appear to be different in greeting people due to the differences in history, cultural traditions and social environments.

   A. 由于在历史、文化传统和社会环境方面的差异,中国人和西方人好像在打招呼时有所不同。

   B. 中国人和西方人由于历史、文化传统和社会环境的原因,在问候时有所不同。

   C. 由于在历史、文化传统和社会环境方面存在差异,中国人和西方人在打招呼时有所不同。

Part Ⅵ   Writing

Task 1

Directions: *Make up a complete sentence by joining the following words.*

1. Mary, got, hair, yellow, has.

2. TV, watching, I, very, much, like.

Unit 1 Campus Life

3. day, every, let's, exercises, do!

4. what, evening, do, shall, this, we?

5. is, experience, mother, of, wisdom, the.

6. college, given, has, life, new, experience, us, a.

7. forward, to, I'm, Shanghai, your, looking, to, coming.

8. here, freshmen, suggestion, is, the, first, for.

Task 2

Directions: *This part is to test your ability to do practical writing. You are required to write a Business card according to the information given below in Chinese.*

实诚电子有限公司

陈　扬

电子工程师

地址：朝阳区岷江路 36 号
电子邮件：cy1978@163.com
电话：010-87652100
手机：13855623234

Unit 2　Pop Music

Part Ⅰ　Listening Comprehension

Task 1

Directions: *In this section you will hear 10 sentences. You are required to circle the word that you hear in brackets.*

1. Jim had two (bucks/books).
2. The sign on the door said: (Poor/Pull).
3. The blue pen looks very (long/lung).
4. In the evening, we should (walk/work) a while.
5. I am (afraid/Africa) not to complete this task.
6. We caught a (beard/bird).
7. We should eat a little (fast/vast) food.
8. Jane (left/leaf) this school two years ago.
9. The little girl's (eyes/ice) are very beautiful.
10. No sooner had I (knack, knocked) than she opened the door.

Task 2

Directions: *In this section you will hear one word from each of the following groups of words. Circle the one you hear.*

1. peak   beak   tick   dick
2. cap   gap   gab   cab
3. curl   girl   pail   bail
4. tale   dale   tear   dear
5. lock   dock   luck   muck
6. took   book   look   cook
7. food   good   would   could
8. turn   burn   learn   mourn
9. shoot   boot   foot   coat
10. pot   hot   lot   cot

Task 3

Directions: This section is to test your ability to give proper responses. There are 5 recorded questions in it. After each question, there is a pause. When you hear a question, you should decide on the correct answer from the 4 choices marked A, B, C and D.

1. A. Yes, he does.   B. No, it isn't.
   C. I'm sorry.   D. Yes, a lot.
2. A. That is true.   B. That is nothing.
   C. Of course. Here you are. D. Yes, there is.
3. A. It's Monday.   B. It's 16th.
   C. It's Mother's Day.   D. It's Children's Day.
4. A. They are balls.   B. It's a schoolboy.
   C. Oh, it's mine.   D. Here you are.
5. A. It looks like Ma Li's. B. My dog is black.
   C. Is it yours?   D. It's lovely.

Task 4

Directions: This section is to test your ability to understand short dialogues. There are 5 recorded dialogues in it. After each dialogue, there is a recorded question. When you hear a question, you should decide on the correct answer from the 4 choices marked A, B, C and D.

Unit 2 Pop Music

1. A. Make a phone call.   B. Buy a book.
   C. Clean the desk.   D. Borrow a pen.
2. A. Asking the way.   B. Booking a room.
   C. Buying a book.   D. Checking in.
3. A. Buy a ticket.   B. Look for Tom.
   C. Call for a doctor.   D. Drive her to the station.
4. A. She likes to do her homework by herself.
   B. She has finished her homework.
   C. She will cook the supper by herself.
   D. She will help the man to cook the supper.
5. A. About eating.   B. Going shopping.
   C. Enjoying a concert.   D. About studying.

Task 5

Directions: *In this section, you will hear a short passage. There are five missing words or phrases in it. Fill in the blanks with the exact words or phrases you hear.*

Why do all these people want to learn English? Why do we learn English? (1)_____ of all, English is one of the world's most widely used languages. It is the international language of (2)_____. It is the language of Britain, the USA, Australia, Canada and so on. Secondly, most books and newspapers are (3)_____ in English. We want to learn high technology from other countries. Thirdly, we want to (4)_____ to other countries, and you can make friends with those who like English and make your life much more colorful. With the help of English, we can (5)_____ with people of many countries.

Part II Dialogue

Task 1

Directions: *Complete the following conversation by making the best choice in the* *table below.*

Li Yu: Look at the boy in the photo. He is a pen pal of mine.

Zhou Yan: How strange he looks! Where is he from?

Li Yu: He is from America. He is of medium height.

Zhou Yan: (1)_____

Li Yu: He is 15 years old. We Chinese teenagers can't color our hair, do you think so?

Zhou Yan: Yeah. And he wears glasses with bright red frames, but he is a boy.

Li Yu: Yeah. Didn't you notice his earring in one ear? It's fun to watch.

Zhou Yan: (2)_____ They might be sorry later.

Li Yu: I agree. Look at his long T-shirt and the big pants just like a big bag.

Zhou Yan: (3)_____ And the picture on the front of the T-shirt looks like a band; he must like the band best.

Li Yu: Yeah. His favorite music is rock. He thinks it's exciting.

Zhou Yan: (4)_____

Li Yu: About once a month. He said he would come to China this summer vacation if he made enough money.

Zhou Yan: Make money?

Li Yu: (5)_____ And he works hard at school, too.

Zhou Yan: I can't imagine he is such a boy. However, in China, we have our own culture.

A: I don't think they should be allowed to do such things.

B. I don't think he is a good student.

C. By the way, how often do you write to him?

D. How old is he? Look at his short hair. It's blue.

E. But I think teenagers should be allowed to choose their own clothes.

F. Teenagers should not be allowed to drive.

G. By taking a part-time job.

Unit 2 Pop Music

Task 2

Directions: *The following are some ways of introducing and identifying people or objects. Read the words spoken and then match them with the functions.*

Words Spoken

A. Who's this? Is it Jack?

B. Hello, Bill, how have you been recently?

C. Mum, this is Mary, my new classmate.

D. It is with great pleasure that I introduce to you Professor Brown, president of Blueville University.

E. Hello! Is Tom there? ... This is Jock speaking.

F. Excuse me, madam. My name is John Smith. I'm from Jingle Bell Company of Beijing.

G. May I present Mr. Brown Close, managing director of ABC Leather Company?

H. Peter, what's that sound? Did you hear it?

I. Who's speaking? Is it Mary?

J. Mary, I'd like you to meet my family. This is my father, ...

Functions

1. Greeting one of your friends. _____

2. Introducing a new classmate to your mother. _____

3. Introducing a guest speaker to audience at a meeting. _____

4. Trying to identify someone. _____

5. Asking someone to identify a sound. _____

6. Introducing oneself at the registration desk of a conference. _____

7. Introducing oneself on the phone. _____

8. Identifying a speaker on the phone. _____

9. Introducing a person very formally. _____

10. Introducing someone to one's family. _____

Part Ⅲ   Vocabulary & Structure

Task 1

Directions: *Tell the basic sentence patterns by choosing the appropriate answer from the 4 choices marked A, B, C and D.*

1. The news is exciting.

   A. sv   B. svo   C. svp   D. svoc

2. He lives in the suburb.

   A. sv   B. svo   C. svp   D. svoo

3. I can't think of his name at the monent.

   A. sv   B. svo   C. svoc   D. svoo

4. He pushed the door open.

   A. sv   B. svp   C. svoc   D. svo

5. Please get me a ticket to the exhibition.

   A. sv   B. svp   C. svoo   D. svo

Directions: *Tell the type of sentence. (simple sentence, compound sentence, complex sentence)*

6. The man knocked at the door.

   A. simple sentence   B. compound sentence   C. complex sentence

7. The man knocked at the door but no one answered.

   A. simple sentence   B. compound sentence   C. complex sentence

8. As soon as he arrived at the house, the man knocked at the door.

   A. simple sentence   B. compound sentence   C. complex sentence

9. We love our great motherland.

   A. simple sentence   B. compound sentence   C. complex sentence

10. Fame, money and position are what he aspires.

    A. simple sentence   B. compound sentence   C. complex sentence

Unit 2　Pop Music

Task 2

Directions: *There are 10 incomplete statements here. You should fill each blank with the proper form of the word given in brackets.*

1. Would you give a detailed _____ of your lost bag? (describe)

2. It's _____ that the average temperature is well above 15 degrees this winter. (normal)

3. By _____ others, the language learners can improve their pronunciation. (imitate)

4. My neighbor, Elizabeth, has a sweet _____ voice. (music)

5. You need _____ to improve your skills. (practice)

6. Despite all our _____ we lost the game 1—0. (effort)

7. No reader is allowed _____ any book out of the library. (take)

8. Last night our manager _____ an email from one supplier about the order. (receive)

9. Those who have IQs over 120 are said to be _____ children. (talent)

10. The internet offers a _____ flow of information. (continue)

Task 3

Directions: *Pay attention to different parts of speech and select the appropriate word to fill in the blanks.*

a. success, succeed, successful

1. You are sure to _____ in food business.

2. The doctor has performed a _____ operation on the patient.

3. It is his interest in the job that leads him to _____.

b. relation, relative, relate

1. She is too proud and doesn't _____ well to her classmates.

2. Many Chinese like to visit friends and _____ during Spring Festival.

3. We have some business _____ with the company.

c. magic, magical, magician

1. The famous singer Wang Fei has a _____ voice and she has many fans.
2. The chemist used a _____ method and mixed several liquids together.
3. Is it easy or difficult to become a _____?

d. wonder, wonderful, wondering

1. I was _____ how you feel about that?
2. We had a _____ time the day before yesterday.
3. The sight of the Great Wall filled us with _____.

e. invent, invention, inventor

1. Who _____ the telephone?
2. Nobody thought that he had turned out a great _____.
3. The _____ of the internet has revolutionized our daily lives.

Task 4

Direction: *Rewrite the following sentences with the expressions in the box.*

| nothing less than | unusual | describe | It turns out that |
| practice | accompany | promptly | be crazy about |

1. Who'd like to give an account of what happened just now?
   _____

2. A reply came without delay.
   _____

3. I have fallen in love with him since the first time I saw him.
   _____

4. Results indicate that with a tiny rewrite this can be achieved.
   _____

Unit 2 Pop Music

5. It was simply a disaster.

_____

6. She continues to learn these skills by repetition in her classroom every day.

_____

7. I must ask you to go to the police station with me.

_____

8. The boy's strange behaviour puzzled the doctor.

_____

Part Ⅳ Reading Comprehension

Task 1

Directions: *Read the following passage and make the correct choice.*

Taiwan police cannot decide whether to treat it as an extremely act of stealing or an even cheat (诈骗). Either way, it would be the perfect crime (犯罪), because the criminals are birds — pigeons!

The crime begins with a telephone message to the owner of a stolen car: if you want the car back, pay up then, the car owner is directed to a park, told where to find a bird cage and how to attach money to the neck of the pigeon inside. Carrying the money in a tiny bag, the pigeon flies off.

There have been at least four such pigeon pick-ups in Changwa. What at first seemed like the work of a clever-at-home car thief, however, may in fact be the work of an even lazier and more inventive criminal mind—one that avoid (避免) not only collecting money but going out to steal the car in the first place. Police officer Chen says that the criminal probably has pulled a double trick: he gets money for things he cannot possibly return. Instead of stealing cars, he lets someone else do it and then waits for the car-owner to place an ad (启事) in the newspaper asking for help.

The theory is supported by the fact that, so far, none of the stolen cars have been returned. Also, the amount of money demanded — under 3,000 Taiwanese dollars — seems too little for a car worth many times more.

　　Demands for pigeon-delivered money stopped as soon as the press reported the story. And even if <u>they</u> start again, Chen holds little hope of catching the criminal. "We have more important things to do," he said.

1. After the car owner received a phone call, he _____.

    A. went to a certain pigeon and put some money in the bag it carried

    B. gave the money to the thief and had his car back in a park

    C. sent some money to the thief by mail

    D. told the press about it

2. The "lazier and more inventive" criminal refers to _____.

    A. the car thief who stays at home

    B. one of those who put the ads in the paper

    C. one of the policemen in Changwa

    D. the owner of the pigeons

3. The writer mentions the fact that "none of the stolen cars have been returned" to show _____.

    A. how easily people get fooled by criminals

    B. what Chen thinks might be correct

    C. the thief is extremely clever

    D. the money paid is too little

4. The underlined word "they" in the last paragraph refers to _____.

    A. criminals   B. pigeons

    C. the stolen cars   D. demands for money

5. We may infer from the text that the criminal knows how to reach the car owners because _____.

    A. he reads the ads in the newspaper

    B. he lives in the same neighbourhood

    C. he has seen the car owners in the park

    D. he has trained the pigeons to follow them

Unit 2 Pop Music

Task 2

Directions: *The following is a list of terms frequently used in music. After reading it, you are required to find the items equivalent to（与……等同）those given in Chinese in the table below.*

A — Country Blues   J — quarter tone
B — rap   K — treble clef
C — Record of the Year   L — marching band
D — rhythm   M — Chopin Serenade
E — timbre   N — key signature
F — Bass Flute   O — light music
G — Piano Concerto   P — folk
H — electronic keyboard   Q — opera house
I — Symphony Hall

Example：四分音(J)   低音长笛(F)
1. 音调符号(   )   轻音乐(   )
2. 乡村布鲁斯(   )   歌剧院(   )
3. 年度最佳唱片(   )   节奏(   )
4. 电子琴(   )   音色(   )
5. 军乐队(   )   现代民歌(   )

Task 3

Directions: *Complete the information by filling in the blanks. Write your answers in no more than 3 words.*

There are many reasons people use checks instead of cash. For one thing, checks are safe to mail. You can pay bills and buy things without worrying. There is no chance that your money will be lost or stolen. Checks are good records, too. Many banks return the checks paid out of your account with your monthly statement.

Sometimes, a bank will not pay your check because you don't have enough money in your account. The check is marked "insufficient funds" and is returned to the person or company to whom you wrote it. If your account is overdrawn, you'll be charged an overdraft (透支) fee. The bank informs you by mail of the overdraft and the resulting charges.

Advantages of Checks
1. (1) ＿＿＿＿＿＿
Pay bills without worrying
2. Your money will not be (2) ＿＿＿.
3. (3) ＿＿＿＿＿＿
Bank's Actions to an Overdraft
4. (4) ＿＿＿＿＿＿ the check
Mark "insufficient funds" on the check
Return the check
5. Charge (5) ＿＿＿＿＿＿
Inform by mail

Task 4

Directions: *Complete the answers in no more than 3 words.*

APPOINTMENTS

YOUNG Italian girl, student, speaks English and French, seeks a post in a school or family, giving lessons or looking after children. — Write Box L. 1367, The Daily—, London, E. C.

YOUNG man, once an officer, tired of uninteresting office work, is willing to go to any part of the world and to do anything legal; speaks several languages; drives all makes of cars; exciting work more important than salary. —Write Box F. 238, The Daily —, London, E. C.

MARRIED couple wanted Gardener; country house 2 miles from Oxford, good bus service; family three adults, five children; wages £ 9; comfortable rooms with central heating. — Write Box S, 754. The Daily —, London, E. C.

1. What kind of work is suitable for the Italian girl?

    Teaching classes or ＿＿＿＿＿＿＿＿.

2. What foreign languages does the Italian girl know?

    She knows ＿＿＿＿＿＿＿＿.

Unit 2 Pop Music

3. Why is the young man tired of his office work?

   Because it is _____.

4. What does the young man think of salary?

   He thinks that salary is _____ than exciting work.

5. What kind of helper are the married couple trying to find?

   They are trying to find _____.

Part Ⅴ Translation

Directions: *This part is to test your ability to translate English into Chinese. Make the best choice.*

1. Adele is simply too magical to compare her to anyone.

   A. 阿黛儿真的是太棒了,没有人可以和她相比。

   B. 阿黛儿真的是太棒了,可以和任何人相比。

   C. 阿黛儿过于神奇了,没有人可以和她相比。

2. She is inarguably one of the biggest female pop stars of all time.

   A. 她不争辩自己一直是最优秀的流行女歌手之一。

   B. 她从不争辩自己是否是最优秀的流行女歌手之一。

   C. 她一直是最优秀的流行女歌手之一,没有人对此质疑。

3. Mozart was a true genius.

   A. 莫扎特是一个真实的天才。

   B. 莫扎特是一个真正的天才。

   C. 莫扎特拥有真正的天赋。

4. To find out whether you should be concerned, it's best to talk to doctors.

   A. 要想知道你是否该关心你身体,最好的办法是和医生谈谈。

   B. 要想知道你是否该关心你身体,最好的办法是询问医生。

   C. 要想知道你是否该担心,最好的办法是和医生谈谈。

5. Mozart's music is played everywhere.
   A. 莫扎特的音乐到处被演奏。
   B. 莫扎特到处演奏音乐。
   C. 莫扎特的音乐无处不在。

6. Personally, I could do without the phone entirely, which makes me unusual.
   A. 我个人认为,完全不用电话我也能过得不错。这点让我与众不同。
   B. 我个人认为,完全不用电话我也能过得不错。这点让我不同寻常。
   C. 我个人认为,完全不用电话我也能做事情。这点让我与众不同。

Part Ⅵ   Writing

Task 1

Directions: *Make up a complete sentence by joining the following words.*

1. have, diary, written, a, you?

2. like, we, to, by, would, bike, go.

3. is, believing, seeing.

4. who, god, help, those, themselves, helps.

5. is, done, half, begun, well.

Unit 2 Pop Music

6. such, must, from, come, heaven, music.

7. we, to, best, do, our, should, achieve, our, in, goal, life.

8. books, the, we, more, learned, the, more, we, become, read.

Task 2

Directions: *This part is to test your ability to do practical writing. You are required to write a gift card according to the information given below in Chinese.*

亲爱的小云：
　　恭喜你喜迁新居，这个花瓶就送给你作为一份小礼物，希望能为你的新家添彩，相信你会喜欢它。
　　祝你在新房子里过得幸福快乐！
　　　　　　　　　　　　　　　　　　　你的好朋友
　　　　　　　　　　　　　　　　　　　小倩

Unit 3 Sports

Part I Listening Comprehension

Task 1

Directions: *In this section you will hear 10 sentences. You are required to circle the word that you hear in brackets.*

1. Look! This (bus/bath) is coming.
2. This (glass/glas) is very cool.
3. Lily said, "We should (sieve/save) time."
4. The (bike/bake) is Jane's.
5. That (boil/boy) looks very handsome.
6. The bell is (ringing/running).
7. Tom's (garage/Gareth) is very large.
8. Please open your (month/mouth) and say "a".
9. (Though/Through) he is great, he must go away.
10. As is (no, known) to the world, China has achieved an economic miracle.

Task 2

Directions: *In this section you will hear one word from each of the following groups of words. Circle the one you hear.*

Unit 3 Sports

1. treasure	measure	pleasure	pressure
2. breathe	breeze	breath	bath
3. father	further	faith	fourth
4. heat	hat	hate	hen
5. kite	late	might	hurt
6. ago	hurt	god	oil
7. lap	sip	dip	map
8. seed	head	board	add
9. peak	tick	leak	lock
10. dad	bad	gap	rap

Task 3

Directions: *This section is to test your ability to give proper responses. There are 5 recorded questions in it. After each question, there is a pause. When you hear a question, you should decide on the correct answer from the 4 choices marked A, B, C and D.*

1. A. Yes tea. B. No I don't like it.
   C. Coffee, please. D. Yes, please.
2. A. Oh, yes. Thank you. B. Very well.
   C. Me, too. D. That's all right.
3. A. Sorry, I don't know her. B. Thanks.
   C. It's too far. D. Across the road.
4. A. It's very interesting. B. OK, no problem.
   C. No, I don't think I need it. D. That's all right.
5. A. I'm feeling very well. B. Don't worry.
   C. It's very hot. D. My car broke down on the way.

Task 4

Directions: *This section is to test your ability to understand short dialogues. There are 5 recorded dialogues in it. After each dialogue, there is a recorded question. When you hear a question, you should decide on the correct*

answer from the 4 choices marked A, B, C and D.

1. A. Washing a car.   B. Asking the way.
   C. Doing some typing.   D. Going out for exercise.
2. A. Pass a letter.   B. See Mr. Smith.
   C. Ask about a question.   D. Talk to Mr. Smith.
3. A. Want to have dinner.   B. Going for dinner.
   C. Don't want to have dinner.   D. Going together.
4. A. In the class.   B. At the office.
   C. At the school gate.   D. In the school.
5. A. She is writing a report.   B. She is reading.
   C. She wants to go out.   D. She has finished it.

Task 5

Directions: *In this section, you will hear a short passage. There are five missing words or phrases in it. Fill in the blanks with the exact words or phrases you hear.*

Canada is a Large country. To the west of it is the Pacific Ocean. To the east is the Atlantic Ocean. Canada is a very (1)_____ country. It is rich in forests, fish, minerals and so on. It is (2)_____ that spread across the country. Most of the tress are evergreen trees. Canada (3)_____ more fish than any other country in the world. There are some very important (4)_____ ores(矿物)in the country. They are iron ore, gold and silver, and coal and oil. Canada has many lakes and rivers. It is easy to make (5)_____ from the water.

Part Ⅱ   Dialogue

Task 1

Directions: *Complete the following conversation by making the best choice in the table below.*

Henry—H   Kitty—K

Unit 3 Sports

H: Hi, Kitty. Are you going to the party tonight?

K: No, I am not (1)_____.

H: You're allowed to go to parties, (2)_____?

K: No. (3)_____ I can't do.

H: Like what?

K: Well, I'm not allowed to (4)_____ on school nights.

H: Really? But there are lots of good shows. You can learn (5)_____

K: Also, I'm not allowed to shop for (6)_____. My mother buys them.

H: Do your parents (7)_____ for you?

K: No, but they have lots of rules.

H: Are you allowed to (8)_____?

K: Oh no! I'm not allowed to have a pet.

H: What are you allowed to do?

K: My parents say I'm allowed to (9)_____. Their rules (10)_____ me a good student.

A. have a pet	B. make
C. allowed	D. There are lots of things
E. clothes	F. aren't you
G. watch TV	H. study all night
I. do everything	J. a lot
K. didn't you	L. books

Task 2

Directions: *The following are some ways of making or responding to suggestions. Read them and match the functions with the words spoken.*

Words Spoken

A. It's all the same to me.

B. Shall we go there by train?

35

C. If I were you, I would buy this dictionary.

D. I don't think that's a good idea.

E. I think your suggestion is acceptable.

F. Can you suggest a better way to deal with this problem?

G. Are you sure it's good?

H. Thank you for your suggestion. That's music to my ears.

I. I'll tell you what — Let's go for a walk.

J. What are the special dishes for today? Can you recommend anything?

Functions

1. You emphasize that your friend's suggestion is just right for you. _____

2. You informally suggest taking a walk. _____

3. Ask whether this idea is okay for the listener. _____

4. You are in a restaurant, talking to a waiter. _____

5. You have doubts about your friend's suggestion. _____

6. Say you would not do the same as the listener. _____

7. Say you don't think much of the suggestion. _____

8. Accept someone else's suggestion. _____

9. Disagree on a suggestion. _____

10. Ask someone to suggest a way to solve a problem. _____

Part Ⅲ Vocabulary & Structure

Task 1

Directions: *Complete each statement by choosing the appropriate answer from the 4 choices marked A, B, C and D.*

1. — The price is fine with me. How would you like _____ paid?

   — Well, it is up to you.

   A. one B. this C. that D. it

Unit 3 Sports

2. The number 9.11 is a special number, _____, I think, that will be remembered by the Americans for ever.

   A. what   B. it   C. which   D. one

3. Thanks to modern irrigation, crops now grow abundantly in areas where once _____ but some bushes could live.

   A. nothing   B. everything C. anything   D. something

4. She asked such a difficult question that I could hardly make any _____ of it at all.

   A. explanation   B. sense   C. meaning   D. idea

5. _____ doesn't seem to have been any difficulty over the money problem.

   A. It   B. That   C. There   D. He

6. I won't want others to know about it. Let's keep it a secret between _____.

   A. I and you   B. you and I
   C. you and me   D. you and him

7. All the Chinese believe Liu Xiang will be the winner of the 110-meter hurdle _____ in the London Olympic.

   A. competition   B. match   C. contest   D. race

8. I have first-hand _____ of taking care of kids.

   A. advice   B. experience C. purpose   D. dream

9. The pupil was more than happy to have got two yuan's _____ of cold drinks from the shop.

   A. worth   B. worthy   C. wealth   D. welfare

10. Used to TV shows, where everything is quick and entertaining, many people do not have the _____ to read a book that requires thinking.

    A. courage   B. wisdom   C. patience   D. freedom

11. _____ are useful animals.

    A. Cow   B. Pig   C. Panda   D. Sheep

12. My _____ of this weekend's activity is going boats with some good friends.

    A. idea   B. purpose   C. mind   D. thought

13. — Is it _____ English dictionary?

— Yes, and it is _____ useful one.

A. a, a B. a, an C. an, an D. an, a

14. — The piano sounds terrible.

— Yes, I want to leave now. Where is the _____?

A. seat B. stage C. exit D. entrance

15. — Please give me a _____ when you arrive in Beijing.

— All right. I'll tell you everything when I get there.

A. newspaper B. ticket C. calling D. ring

Task 2

Directions: *There are 10 incomplete statements here. You should fill each blank with the proper form of the word given in brackets.*

1. The combination of the two companies would greatly improve their _____ and position in the international market. (compete)

2. This machine can be connected _____ to the computer. (external)

3. Those shoes she bought yesterday were _____ cheap. (amaze)

4. We take great _____ in providing our professional services and hospitality. (proud)

5. It is your _____ duty to vote in the local elections. (civic)

6. It was a _____ not to be missed. (spectacle)

7. We invited a number of minor _____. (celebrity)

8. I can't _____ her to be on time if I'm late myself. (expectation)

9. To meet the customers' _____, we provide a great variety of services. (require)

10. Some companies prefer experienced and _____ employees. (skill)

Task 3

Directions: *Pay attention to different parts of speech and select the appropriate word to fill in the blanks.*

a. comfort, comfortable, comfortably

Unit 3 Sports

1. Very soon, all the campers were settled _____.
2. Our hotel will provide you with _____ stay.
3. There is plenty of room to lie down and you can sleep in _____.

b. oppose, opposite, opposing

1. There is a big supermarket on the _____ side of the street.
2. Most residents _____ pulling down the building.
3. I don't like the way he solves problems, so I cast an _____ vote.

c. expect, expectation, unexpected

1. His death was totally _____.
2. I _____ to be back within a week.
3. Tom has succeeded beyond my _____.

d. celebrate, celebrity, celebrities

1. He's a national _____.
2. Sports _____ is a high income group.
3. How do you usually _____ New Year?

e. compete, competitor, competitive

1. More and more athletes from different countries _____ in modern Olympic Games.
2. All _____ are required to arrive two days in advance.
3. The job market is so _____ and you should make preparations for it.

Task 4

Direction: *Rewrite the following sentences with the expressions in the box.*

| all of a sudden | loads of | go on | root for |
| tune in | | dress up | look up to | be proud of |

1. He has got lots of money.

2. I suddenly remembered that I hadn't locked the door.

3. Children should respect their parents.

4. We take great pride in offering the best service in town.

5. They came to the baseball field to support their school team.

6. The church is being held a wedding.

7. We shall decorate the hall for the National Day.

8. Listen to BBC tonight at 9 o'clock.

Part Ⅳ Reading Comprehension

Task 1

Directions*: Read the following passage and make the correct choice.*

In modern society there is a great deal of argument about competition. Some value it highly, believing that it is responsible for social progress and prosperity. Others say that competition is bad; that it sets one person against another; that it leads to unfriendly relationship between people.

I have taught many children who held the belief that their self-worth relied (依赖) on how well they performed at tennis and other skills. For them, playing well and winning are often life-and-death affairs. In their single-minded pursuit

Unit 3 Sports

（追求） of success, the development, of many other human qualities is certainly forgotten.

However, while some seem to be lost in the desire to succeed, others take an opposite attitude. In a culture which values only the winner and pays no attention to the ordinary players, they strongly blame competition. Among <u>the most vocal</u> are young-stars who have suffered under competitive pressures from their parents or society. Teaching these young people, I often observe in them a desire to fail. They seem to seek failure by not trying to win or achieve success. By not trying, they always have an excuse: "I may have lost, but it doesn't matter because I really didn't try." What is not usually admitted by themselves is the belief that if they had really tried and lost, that would mean a lot. Such a loss would be a measure of their worth. Clearly, this belief is the same as that of the true competitors who try to prove themselves. Both are based on the mistaken belief that one's self-respect relies on how well one performs in comparison with others. Both are afraid of not being valued. Only as this basic and often troublesome fear begins to dissolve(缓解) can we discover a new meaning in competition.

1. What does this passage mainly talk about?
    A. Competition helps to set up self-respect.
    B. Opinions about competition are different among people.
    C. Competition is harmful to personal quality development.
    D. Failures are necessary experiences in competition.
2. Why do some people favor competition according to the passage?
    A. It pushes society forward.
    B. It builds up a sense of duty.
    C. It improves personal abilities.
    D. It encourages individual efforts.
3. The underlined phrase "the most vocal" in Paragraph 3 means _____.
    A. those who try their best to win
    B. those who value competition most strongly
    C. those who are against competition most strongly
    D. those who rely on others most for success
4. What is the similar belief of the true competition and those with a "desire to fail"?

A. One's worth lies in his performance compared with others.

B. One's success in competition needs great efforts.

C. One's achievement is determined by his particular skills.

D. One's success is based on how hard he has tried.

5. Which point of view may the author agree to?

A. Every effort should be paid back.

B. Competition should be encouraged.

C. Winning should be a life-and-death matter.

D. Fear of failure should be removed in competition.

Task 2

Directions: *The following is a list of terms frequently used in sports. After reading it, you are required to find the items equivalent to（与……等同）those given in Chinese in the table below.*

A — track meet

B — pole vault

C — heptathlon

D — shot put

E — long jump

F — men's singles

G — mixed doubles

H — beach volleyball

I — freestyle

J — freestyle relay

K — medley relay

L — 10m platform event

M — rhythmic gymnastics

N — pommel horse

O — time trial

P — clean and jerk

Q — team events

Example：跳远（E）　　　　十米跳台（L）

1. 撑竿跳高（　　）　　　沙滩排球（　　）

2. 混合泳接力（　　）　　挺举（　　）

3. 计时赛（　　）　　　　团体赛（　　）

4. 男子单打（　　）　　　艺术体操（　　）

5. 田径运动会（　　）　　鞍马（　　）

Unit 3 Sports

Task 3

Directions: *Complete the information by filling in the blanks. Write your answers in no more than 3 words.*

Most meetings have an agenda (议事日程). For a formal meeting, this document may be handed out in advance to all participants. For an informal meeting, the agenda may be simply a list of the points to be dealt with. The purpose of an agenda is to speed up the meeting and keep everyone to the point. The agenda for a formal meeting must be organized in logical order. Often the agenda shows not only the topics but the meeting's function concerning each line. All items on which a decision is to be taken should appear on the agenda.

One-to-one or small informal meetings also tend to be structured and planned. They are different from chance conversations in a corridor or over coffee. Small informal meetings may also take place or continue during a meal.

1. Most meetings have (1) _____.
2. The document may be handed out (2) _____ to all participants.
3. The purpose of an agenda is to (3) _____ the meeting and keep every one to the point.
4. The agenda shows both (4) _____ and (5) _____ concerning each line.

Task 4

Directions: *Complete the answers in no more than 3 words.*

Ad 1

Personal Assistant To Sales Manager

We are a small but growing computer software company. We are looking for someone to assist the manager of the sales department in dealing with foreign customers and orders from abroad. If you know English well and have previous experience in this job, and between 21 and 30, please write us a short letter giving details of your previous jobs, current employment, etc. Some knowledge of Spanish and

Italian would be an advantage.

Write to:

Soft Logic

23 Alfred Street

Winchester

Hants

Ad 2

Part time Drivers

King County Metro is Hiring Part-Time Bus Drivers

Great Pay! Great Benefits!

Start at MYM14.50 an hour.

Plus paid vacation and sick leave, paid training.

Must be 21 years or older, have a Washington State driver's license and acceptable driving record.

Call (202)684-1024

Or log onto (登录) www.metrokc.gov/ohrm

1. In the first ad. which department in the company is seeking an assistant to its manager?
   _____.

2. What is the major responsibility of the assistant manager?
   Dealing with foreign customers and orders _____.

3. What is mentioned as an advantage for the application in Ad 1?
   Some knowledge of _____.

4. What is the age limit for the position of the part-time bus drivers in Ad 2?
   _____ years or older.

5. What kind of driver's license should the candidates have in order to get the position?
   They should have a _____ driver's license.

Unit 3 Sports

Part Ⅴ Translation

Directions: *This part is to test your ability to translate English into Chinese. Make the best choice and write the translation of the paragraph.*

1. All of a sudden, you are among athletes you look up to.

    A. 你一下子就置身于你仰慕的运动员之中。

    B. 你突然就很崇拜这些运动员。

    C. 你突然抬头就看到了这些运动员。

2. Fans often dress up in their team's jerseys. Some even paint their faces with the team's colors.

    A. 粉丝们经常会穿着支持方的队服。有些粉丝甚至在他们的脸上涂上支持方的色彩。

    B. 粉丝们用球队的服装来装扮自己。有些甚至还在脸上涂上五颜六色。

    C. 粉丝们总是穿上队服。有的粉丝甚至在脸上涂上国旗。

3. Because the telephone is changing our lives more than any other piece of technology.

    A. 因为电话比其他任何一项技术都更大地改变了我们的生活。

    B. 因为电话正在改变我们的生活,比其他任何一项技术改变得都大。

    C. 因为是电话改变我们的生活而不是其他任何一项技术。

4. Paul is a typical learner of English with a generally low level of motivation.

    A. 保罗是个英语学习动机很低的典型学习者。

    B. 保罗是个具有低水平英语学习动机的典型学生。

    C. 保罗是个典型的英语学习动机很低的学生。

5. The Super Bowl gives people across the country a good reason to celebrate.

    A. "超级杯"有理由让人们在全国庆祝。

B. "超级杯"有理由给人们去全国各地庆祝。

C. "超级杯"让全国人有了庆祝的好理由。

6. Thanks to the efforts of those professionals, we can always know the weather in advance and get prepared for it.

A. 谢谢那些专家们的努力,我们能够总是知道天气提前为它做好准备。

B. 多谢那些专家们的努力,我们总能提前知道天气情况并为此做好准备。

C. 多亏那些专家们的努力,我们总能提前知道天气情况并为此做好准备。

Part Ⅵ Writing

Task 1

Directions: *Make up a complete sentence by joining the following words.*

1. it, invention, is, revolutionary, a.

2. health, overwork, harm, does, to.

3. good, reading, does, to, mind, our.

4. the Super Bowl, the biggest, game, football, is, of the year.

5. seen, I, since, graduated, haven't, you, we.

6. great, smoking, health, influence, has, a, on, our.

Unit 3 Sports

7. given, gold, will, best, be, to, the, athletes, medals.

8. the, football game, of the year, brings, biggest, high, expectations.

Task 2

Directions: *This part is to test your ability to do practical writing. You are required to write a Lost and Found Announcement according to the information given below in Chinese.*

> 失物招领
>
> 　　有人在商场内捡到手表一块，交至本室。丢表者请带身份证前来认领，特此公告。
>
> 　　　　　　　　　　　　　　　　　　　　　失物招领办公室

Unit 4　Food Culture

Part I　Listening Comprehension

Task 1

Directions: *In this section you will hear 10 sentences. You are required to circle the word that you hear in brackets.*

1. A (year's/ear's) plan starts with spring.
2. All is (fare/fair) in war.
3. Prevention is better than the (cure/curl).
4. A (cloth/close) mouth catches no flies.
5. A (sound/sun) ruined is in a sound body.
6. Reason (rules/roles) all things.
7. As the (tree/train), so the fruit.
8. (Draw/Drop) water with a sieve.
9. Has the (daughter, doctor) arrived?
10. Harm (watch/wash), harm catch.

Task 2

Directions: *In this section you will hear one word from each of the following groups of words. Circle the one you hear.*

Unit 4 Food Culture

1. tear   year   pierce   pear
2. pear   fair   mayor   air
3. cure   poor   pour   sure
4. know   bureau   dome   most
5. loud   browser   count   found
6. wrap   rust   wrist   rest
7. trial   try   trap   treat
8. fetch   chip   chap   chop
9. cage   mage   message   merge
10. weak   window   wax   widen

Task 3

Directions: *This section is to test your ability to give proper responses. There are 5 recorded questions in it. After each question, there is a pause. When you hear a question, you should decide on the correct answer from the 4 choices marked A, B, C and D.*

1. A. Don't worry.   B. Never mind.
   C. I'm fine, thanks.   D. It's a pity.
2. A. At 3 p.m.   B. A week before.
   C. 12 hours.   D. Not very long.
3. A. It's very well.   B. I don't think so.
   C. Don't do that.   D. Oh, no.
4. A. Right!   B. I have a headache.
   C. It's expensive.   D. I have no time.
5. A. I help you.   B. Yes, I'd like to order that.
   C. It's expensive.   D. Of course not.

Task 4

Directions: *This section is to test your ability to understand short dialogues. There are 5 recorded dialogues in it. After each dialogue, there is a recorded question. When you hear a question, you should decide on the correct*

49

answer from the 4 choices marked A, B, C and D.

1. A. Agree to.   B. He has no time.
   C. Not bad.   D. I can't dance.
2. A. Have a cold.   B. Catching bus.
   C. Afraid of the exam. D. No courage.
3. A. Have breakfast.   B. Having bread.
   C. Have a rest.   D. Have dinner.
4. A. At 10:13   B. At 10:30
   C. At 10:00   D. At 12:30
5. A. Like music.   B. Like singing.
   C. Like dancing.   D. Like movie.

Task 5

Directions: *In this section, you will hear a short passage. There are five missing words or phrases in it. Fill in the blanks with the exact words or phrases you hear.*

I like to use my bicycle for short journeys. It is (1)_____ than waiting for a bus. On my bike I can get a lot of exercises and fresh air, and this can make me happy and feel younger.

If you live in a big city, it is often faster than a car. You can leave your bike anywhere, so you needn't worry about (2)_____. The bike needn't use (3)_____, gas or any other fuel. So we have been (4)_____ the benefits of cycling for years. So bikes are good for our city or town, do you think so?

I use it most in summer, autumn, spring when the weather is warm and dry. Of course it can be (5)_____ in winter, for it is cold and often the rain is heavy.

Part II   Dialogue

Task 1

Directions: *Complete the following conversation by making the best choice in the*

Unit 4 Food Culture

table below.

A: Jack, I've been asked to a dinner party tonight. What time should I arrive for that?

B: (1)_____

A: Yes, they did. They said seven.

B: Then get there at seven fifteen. (2)_____

A: Why so?

B: That's just what it is here. Maybe the hostess is still busy getting ready for the dinner.

A: What will happen if I can't get there in time?

B: (3)_____ And if you really arrive late, say "sorry" as soon as you arrive and then do not worry about it.

A: What should I bring? (4) _____ I certainly can't go there empty-handed.

B: For the first time, you could bring a small present. You don't want to show how rich you are, do you?

A: No, certainly not.

B: (5) _____

A: No, thanks very much.

    A. You must call and say you will be late.
    B. You are very busy.
    C. Didn't they tell you when the party will start?
    D. Any more questions?
    E. I mean what present I should take.
    F. Just make sure you're later than the time.
    G. That's enough for you to walk there.

Task 2

Directions: *The following are some ways of making offers and responding to* them. Read them and match the functions with the words spoken.

Words Spoken

A. That's very kind of you, thank you.

B. Should I get you a glass of water?

C. No, don't bother. I can do it myself.

D. I wonder if I might order some dessert for you.

E. I think I can manage, but thank you for asking.

F. Thanks anyway.

G. Let me try to work it out

H. What can I do for you?

I. It's a once-in-a-lifetime offer.

J. Thank you all the same.

Functions

1. You offer to solve a problem. _____

2. You thank someone even though their offer didn't help. _____

3. You don't want to bother someone because you can do it yourself. _____

4. You express thanks for someone's offer. _____

5. You are trying to persuade someone to accept your offer. _____

6. You want to offer help to somebody. _____

7. You tentatively offer to order some dessert for your friend. _____

8. You offer to get a drink for your friend. _____

9. You thank someone for his/her kindness. _____

10. You thank someone even though you don't need their help. _____

Part Ⅲ   Vocabulary & Structure

Task 1

Directions: Complete each statement by choosing the appropriate answer from the 4 choices marked A, B, C and D.

Unit 4 Food Culture

1. John has three sisters. Mary is the _____ of the three.
   A. most cleverest   B. more clever   C. cleverest   D. cleverer
2. The students are _____ young people between the age of sixteen and twenty.
   A. most   B. mostly   C. almost   D. at most
3. She told us _____ story that we all forgot about the time.
   A. such an interesting   B. such interesting a
   C. so an interesting   D. a so interesting
4. It is impossible for so _____ workers to do so _____ work in a single day.
   A. few, much   B. few, many
   C. little, much   D. little, many
5. The horse is getting old and can't run _____ it did.
   A. as faster as   B. so fast than
   C. so faster as   D. as fast as
6. The story sounds _____.
   A. to be true   B. as true
   C. being true   D. true
7. I'd been expecting _____ letters the whole morning, but there weren't _____ for me.
   A. some; any   B. many; a few
   C. some; one   D. a few; none
8. This year they have produced _____ grain _____ they did last year.
   A. as less; as   B. as few; as
   C. less; than   D. fewer; than
9. After the new technique was introduced, the factory produced _____ tractors in 1988 as the year before.
   A. as twice many   B. as many twice
   C. twice as many   D. twice many as

10. The pianos in the other shop will be _____, but _____.

   A. cheaper; not as better   B. cheaper; not as good

   C. more cheaper; not as better   D. more cheap; not as good

11. Cindy likes to tell jokes. She never stops talking. She is _____.

   A. serious   B. quiet   C. shy   D. outgoing

12. — This digital camera is really cheap.

   — The _____ the better. I'm short of money, you see.

   A. cheap   B. cheaper

   C. expensive   D. more expensive

13. Pass my glasses to me, Jack. I can _____ read the words in the newspaper.

   A. hardly   B. really   C. rather   D. clearly

14. Sixteen-year-olds aren't _____ at that age.

   A. enough serious   B. serious enough

   C. seriously enough   D. enough seriously

15. — The smell in the room is really terrible.

   — You said it. Let's keep all the windows _____.

   A. closed   B. open   C. opening   D. to open

Task 2

Directions: *There are 10 incomplete statements here. You should fill each blank with the proper form of the word given in brackets.*

1. It is important to look at the novel in its _____ context. (history)

2. Martin Luther King's famous speech was very _____. (inspire)

3. Like many New Yorkers, he had a _____ image of country life. (romance)

4. The body can _____ itself to changes of temperature. (adjust)

5. If you don't want to be disturbed, you can have your telephone _____. (connect)

6. These shoes are _____ made for the disabled. (special)

7. This job involves _____, artistic talent, good communication skills and

Unit 4 Food Culture

computer skills. (create)

8. What do you think of the _____ meat? (preserve)

9. All _____ on the weather. (depend)

10. Successful people often aren't very good at dealing with _____. (fail)

Task 3

Directions: *Pay attention to different parts of speech and select the appropriate word to fill in the blanks.*

a. like, alike, likely

1. It is _____ to rain.

2. My mother and I are _____ in many ways.

3. How do you _____ this play?

b. create, creative, creation

1. Man is _____ equal.

2. American education focuses on students' _____ thinking.

3. The _____ of a new playground will benefit the children a lot.

c. tradition, traditional, traditionally

1. Christmas and Thanks-giving Day are most important _____ holidays in America.

2. _____, most Chinese give their house a thorough cleaning before Spring Festival.

3. According to _____, it's the bride's parents who pay for the wedding.

d. preserve, preserved, preserver

1. This is a life _____.

2. Duck eggs do not _____ satisfactorily.

3. These books are well _____!

e. able, unable, capable

1. _____ to sleep, I got up and made myself a drink.
2. Mary is the most _____ girl I have ever known.
3. The classroom is _____ of seating 50 students.

Task 4

Direction: *Rewrite the following sentences with the expressions in the box.*

| hear from | because of | superior | insist on |
| decide to | a delicacy | not only... but also... | set out to |

1. The government has begun to make many needed reforms.
   _____

2. Thanks to your help, we were successful.
   _____

3. Snails are considered delicious food in France.
   _____

4. He speaks both English and Japanese.
   _____

5. If you do make up your mind to use it, what would you do with it?
   _____

6. She adhered to leaving at once.
   _____

7. The book is better than that.
   _____

8. I look forward to receiving a letter from you.
   _____

Unit 4 Food Culture

Part IV Reading Comprehension

Task 1

***Directions:** Read the following passage and make the correct choice.*

There seems never to have been a civilization without toys, but when and how they developed is unknown. They probably came about just to give children something to do.

In the ancient world, as is today, most boys played with some kinds of toys and most girls with another. In societies where social roles are rigidly determined, boys pattern their play after the activities of their fathers and girls after the tasks of their mothers. This is true because boys and girls are being prepared, even in play, to step into the roles and responsibilities of the adult world.

What is remarkable about the history of toys is not so much how they changed over the centuries but how much they have remained the same. The changes have been mostly in terms of craftsmanship, mechanics, and technology. It is the universality of toys with regard to their development in all parts of the world and their persistence to the present that is amazing. In Egypt, America, China, Japan and among the Arctic peoples, generally the same kinds of toys appeared. Variations depended on local customs and ways of life because toys imitate their surroundings. Nearly every civilization had dolls, little weapons, toy soldiers, tiny animals and vehicles.

Because toys can generally be regarded as a kind of art form, they have not been subject to technological leaps that characterize inventions for adult use. The progress from the wheel to the oxcart (牛车) to the automobile is a direct line of ascent (进步). The progress from a rattle (拨浪鼓) used by inventiveness. Each rattle is the product of the artistic tastes of times and subject to the limitations of available materials.

1. The reason why the toys most boys play with are different from those that girls play with is that _____.

A. boys like to play with their fathers while girls with their mothers

   B. they like challenging-activities

   C. their social roles are rigidly determined

   D. most boys would like to follow their fathers' professions

2. What is particular about the history of toys?

   A. They changed over the centuries.

   B. They are improved by technological advances.

   C. They are quite different in different countries.

   D. They are almost the same all over the world.

3. The word "universality" in Paragraph 3 means _____.

   A. common   B. difference

   C. interest   D. endurance

4. Regarded as a kind of art form, toys _____.

   A. reflect the social progress

   B. follow a direct line of ascent

   C. are losing appeals to adults

   D. are not characterized by technological progress

5. The author used the example of a rattle to show that _____.

   A. even a simple toy can mirror the artistic tastes of the time

   B. in toy-making there is a continuity in the use of materials

   C. even the simplest toys can reflect the progress of technology

   D. it often takes a long time to introduce new technology into toy-making

Task 2

Directions: The following is a list of terms frequently used in restaurants. After reading it, you are required to find the items equivalent to (与……等同) those given in Chinese in the table below.

A — fried egg   E — salted duck egg

B — dim sum   F — soybean milk

C — scramble egg   G — instant-boiled mutton

D — clay oven rolls   H — sliced noodles

Unit 4 Food Culture

I — rice noodles
J — spicy hot noodles
K — seaweed soup
L — egg & vegetable soup
M — fish ball soup

N — boiled dumplings
O — pudding
P — mashed potatoes
Q — rice and vegetable roll

Example：豆浆(F)   米粉(I)
1. 饭团(   )   水饺(   )
2. 麻辣面(   )   布丁(   )
3. 紫菜汤(   )   蛋花汤(   )
4. 鱼丸汤(   )   烧饼(   )
5. 涮羊肉(   )   咸鸭蛋(   )

Task 3

Directions: *Complete the information by filling in the blanks. Write your answers in no more than 3 words.*

Dear Brain Store Customer,

　　We hope you enjoyed books and other items included in our catalogue (目录). Whether you're a teacher, trainer, or parent, we're sure you will find hundreds of valuable teaching and learning resources here.

　　When your decisions are made, we'll do the rest. We accept orders by mail, phone, fax and online at www. thebrainstore. com. Based on available stock, your order will be delivered within two business days.

　　Since we are personally committed to your total satisfaction, any Brain Store product sold is guaranteed for 90 days. Please call 800-325-4896 for additional information. Our friendly Customer Service Office is to answer all of your questions. Feel free to call us between 8:00 a. m. and 4:30 p. m., Pacific Standard Time, Monday through Friday or email us at info@thebrainstore.com.

Information About a Bookstore
Name of the book store: (1) _____
Delivery period: (2) _____
Orders can be accepted by
1) mail   2) (3) _____   3) (4) _____
4) and online at www.thebrainstore.com
Guarantee period: (5) _____

Task 4

***Directions**: Complete the answers in no more than 3 words.*

Almost every family buys at least one copy of newspaper every day. Some people subscribe (订购) to as many as two or three different newspapers. But why do people read newspaper?

Five hundred years ago, news of important happenings — battles lost and won, kings or rulers overthrown or killed — took months to travel from one country to another. The news passed by word of mouth and was never accurate. Today we can read in our newspapers of important events that occur in faraway countries on the same day they happen.

Apart from supplying news from all over the world, newspapers give us a lot of other useful information. There are weather reports, radio, television and film guides, book reviews, stories, and, of course, advertisements. There are all sorts of advertisements. The bigger ones are put in by large companies to bring attention to their products. They pay the newspapers thousands of dollars for the advertising space, but it is worth the money for news of their products goes into almost every home in the country. For those who produce newspapers, advertisements are also very important. Money earned from advertisements makes it possible for them to sell their newspaper at a low price and still make profit.

1. How do people get newspapers today?

   By _____ newspapers.

2. How was important news sent to different places in the past?

Unit 4　Food Culture

　　It was sent by ＿＿＿＿＿＿＿＿＿＿．

3. What is the most important function of a newspaper, apart from the news?

　　＿＿＿＿＿＿＿＿＿＿．

4. Why do people advertise on newspaper?

　　Because news of their products will ＿＿＿＿＿＿＿＿＿＿．

5. What is the reason for newspapers to carry a lot of advertisements?

　　To lower the price and ＿＿＿＿＿＿＿＿＿＿．

Part Ⅴ　Translation

Directions: *This part is to test your ability to translate English into Chinese. Make the best choice and write the translation of the paragraph.*

1. Every day we go to work hoping to do two things: share the great coffee with our friends and help make the world a little better.

　　A. 我们每天上班都期待两件事：与朋友一起喝喝美妙的咖啡和为世界做一份贡献。

　　B. 我们每天上班都期待两件事：分享朋友美妙的咖啡和为世界做一份贡献。

　　C. 我们每天上班都期待两件事：与朋友一起喝喝美妙的咖啡和生活得好一点。

2. To this day, Haagen-Dazs remains committed to developing exceptional new super premium frozen dessert experience.

　　A. 直到今天，哈根达斯仍然致力于开发独特的、一流的冷饮体验。

　　B. 直到今天，哈根达斯仍然承诺开发独特的、一流的冷饮体验。

　　C. 直到今天，哈根达斯仍然致力于开发独特的、一流的冷饮新体验。

3. I must study cleverly to obtain more knowledge.

　　A. 我必须学习聪明地获得更多的知识。

　　B. 我必须学习巧妙地获得更多的知识。

　　C. 我必须巧妙地学习以获得更多的知识。

4. It's all a matter of perception.

   A. 它全部就是一个感知性的问题而已。

   B. 这都是一个理解上的偏差。

   C. 这就是一个洞察力的问题。

5. We should focus on a balanced diet, which assures us the necessary nutrition.

   A. 我们应该把焦点放在饮食平衡上，这能保证我们必要的营养。

   B. 我们应该注意饮食平衡，这能保证我们必要的营养。

   C. 因为它能保证我们必要的营养，所以我们应该注意饮食平衡。

6. I will give you a clear idea of the market conditions in the region as soon as possible.

   A. 我会尽快让你们清楚地了解该地区的市场情况。

   B. 我将尽可能设法弄清楚该地区的市场销售情况。

   C. 我会尽早向你们清楚地说明该地区的市场情况。

Part Ⅵ　Writing

Task 1

Directions: *Make up a complete sentence by joining the following words.*

1. requires, the, patience, great, job.

2. that's, it, why, don't, reason, the, I, like.

3. a, the, machine, is, wonderful, computer.

Unit 4 Food Culture

4. music, listening, to, us, relaxed, to, feel, enables.

5. any, menu, on, fish, there, is, the.

6. a journey, a single step, a thousand, begins, with, of, miles.

7. speak, than, louder, actions, words.

8. what, what, do, do, you, you, say, say.

Task 2

Directions: *This part is to test your ability to do practical writing. You are required to write a note according to the information given below in Chinese.*

> 说明：假设你是肖亮，给方主任 Dean Fang 写一张请假条。
> 时间：2012 年 4 月 26 日
> 1. 得了重感冒，想请假去医院看病；
> 2. 想请假两天，时间 4 月 26 日到 27 日；
> 3. 如果您准假，我将不胜感激；
> 4. 期间落下的功课，回来将尽快补上。

Unit 5　Movie

Part Ⅰ　Listening Comprehension

Task 1

Directions: *In this section you will hear 10 sentences. You are required to circle the word that you hear in brackets.*

1. We saw the (cup/cop).
2. Better (wit/wet) than wealth.
3. (Ears/Years) bring wisdom.
4. Merry (meet/met), merry part.
5. (Learn/Lean) to walk before you can run.
6. A tree is known by (its/eats) fruit.
7. Doing is better than (saying/seeing).
8. He (through/threw) the ball up and caught it again.
9. There are a thousand and (won/one) stars in the sky.
10. It's all (right/write) to borrow money occasionally, but don't let it become a habit.

Task 2

Directions: *In this section you will hear one word from each of the following*

Unit 5 Movie

groups of words. Circle the one you hear.

1. walk   weak   word   work
2. yawn   unit   yield   just
3. arm   form   palm   beam
4. dine   crown   bean   fine
5. down   dumpling   ring   amusing
6. cats   pets   boats   charts
7. beds   roads   needs   hands
8. lawn   lease   lord   lump
9. month   mouth   mouse   mores
10. slow   snow   slob   snob

Task 3

Directions: *This section is to test your ability to give proper responses. There are 5 recorded questions in it. After each question, there is a pause. When you hear a question, you should decide on the correct answer from the 4 choices marked A, B, C and D.*

1. A. Here you are.   B. A pen on the desk.
   C. Oh, yes, it is.   D. Yes, it is a nice pen.
2. A. I am.   B. I am a teacher.
   C. Mr Wang is there.   D. It doesn't matter.
3. A. Going to a factory   B. Great! This is going to be fun.
   C. You have to.   D. Bye-bye
4. A. Yes, I do.   B. She is well.
   C. I'm a typewriter.   D. I'm reading.
5. A. I have no idea. What about you?   B. Meet at six.
   C. Give up.   D. Come on.

Task 4

Directions: *This section is to test your ability to understand short dialogues. There are 5 recorded dialogues in it. After each dialogue, there is a recorded*

65

question. When you hear a question, you should decide on the correct answer from the 4 choices marked A, B, C and D.

1. A. About a boy. B. About students.
   C. About an article by a girl. D. About college.
2. A. By bus. B. Traveling.
   C. They can take a bus to the Palace. D. By taxi.
3. A. Room 540. B. Room 405.
   C. Room 450. D. Room 504.
4. A. At home. B. At school.
   C. At hospital. D. In class.
5. A. Sour cream. B. Milk
   C. Like fruit. D. Savory food.

Task 5

Directions: *In this section, you will hear a short passage. There are five missing words or phrases in it. Fill in the blanks with the exact words or phrases you hear.*

Shopping for clothes is not the same (1) _____ for a man as it is for a woman. A man goes shopping because he needs something. He knows what he wants. His object is to find it and (2) _____ it, but the price isn't the first consideration. Next let's see a woman shops in the opposite way. Her shopping is not often (3) _____ on need. She usually hasn't made up her mind what she wants, so she is only "having a look around". Faced with a roomful of dresses, a woman can (4) _____ an hour easily going from one rack to another, while few men have the same (5)_____.

Part II　Dialogue

Task 1

Directions: *Complete the following conversation by making the best choice in the*

Unit 5 Movie

   table below.

A: (1)_____ I was wondering if you are free tomorrow night.

B: Well, Lucy. (2)_____

A: I've just got a pair of Seoul Riders movie tickets and (3)_____ if you can come along. (4)_____

B: That sounds great! (5)_____

A: No problem. My pleasure.

B: I really wanted to go to see the film, (6)_____ How did you get the tickets?

A: A friend of mine gave them to me.

B: Oh, (7)_____ I'm so excited. So when are we going?

A: (8)_____ The movie starts at seven pm. (9)_____ because there'll be a big line.

B: OK. Good.

A: OK. (10)_____

> A. you are so lucky!
> B. Would you like to go?
> C. Well, let's see.
> D. But the tickets were sold out.
> E. Why do you ask that?
> F. Hi, Lily!
> G. We should get there at least one hour earlier,
> H. I don't know
> I. Thanks for inviting me!
> J. See you tomorrow!

Task 2

Directions: *The following are some ways of asking for and giving permission. Read the words spoken and then match them with the functions.*

Words Spoken

A. Do you mind if I turn up the radio?

B. By all means.

C. Any one mind if I turn off the light?

D. Sure, go ahead.

E. May I sit here?

F. I'm afraid that'll be impossible.

G. I was wondering if I could bring a friend to your birthday party.

H. I don't mind, do it if you like.

I. Will it be possible for me to take a day off tomorrow?

Functions

1. You politely ask for permission to bring a friend to a party. _____

2. The sentence for asking for permission. _____

3. The sentence for giving permission. _____

4. You give permission in an informal way. _____

5. You politely refuse to give permission. _____

6. You allow your friend to do what he wants to. _____

7. You ask for permission to sit down. _____

8. You tentatively ask for a day off. _____

9. You politely ask if you can turn up the radio louder. _____

Part Ⅲ　Vocabulary & Structure

Task 1

Directions: Complete each statement by choosing the appropriate answer from the 4 choices marked A, B, C and D.

1. If you do not feel well, you should not _____ going to see a doctor.

　　A. pick out　　　　　　　　B. give off

　　C. put off　　　　　　　　 D. make out

Unit 5　Movie

2. A good writer must _____ what he writes with what has happened around him.

   A. connect　　　B. think　　　C. join　　　D. know

3. We want our children to know that hard work _____.

   A. comes off　　　　　　　B. gives off

   C. pays off　　　　　　　D. sees off

4. We can't wait. We have to _____ the direction and the distance before we take action.

   A. pull out　　　　　　　B. figure out

   C. think out　　　　　　　D. turn out

5. — I don't know if Mr Wang _____ to the party this evening.

   — I think he will come if he _____ free.

   A. will come; will be　　　B. comes; is

   C. comes; will be　　　　D. will come; is

6. She went into her room, _____ the light and began to study.

   A. turned up　　　B. turned on　　　C. turned down　　　D. turned off

7. We _____ what we have said at the meeting.

   A. lead to　　　B. see to　　　C. get to　　　D. hold to

8. — Your tie looks smart. It _____ with your shirt perfectly.

   — Thanks. I'm glad you like it.

   A. suits　　　B. meets　　　C. agrees　　　D. goes

9. She had a kind nature, so that she quickly _____ the friendship of her classmates.

   A. made　　　B. won　　　C. caught　　　D. seized

10. — Must I get up early tomorrow morning?

    — No, _____.

    A. I don't think you have to　　　B. you mustn't

    C. you can't　　　　　　　　　D. you needn't

11. Can we _____ this magazine for two hours?

    A. borrow　　　B. lend　　　C. keep　　　D. take

12. — Have you heard the song "Take Me to Your Heart"?

    — Yes, it _____ terrific.

  A. smells   B. sounds   C. listens   D. hears

13. — May I go now?

  — No. You _____ let the teacher know first.

  A. need   B. must   C. can't   D. may

14. The ice cream tasted so _____ that the kids asked for some more.

  A. bad   B. badly   C. delicious   D. well

15. Excuse me. May I _____ you to pass me the book?

  A. keep   B. make   C. get   D. trouble

Task 2

Directions: *There are 10 incomplete statements here. You should fill each blank with the proper form of the word given in brackets.*

1. The room still has many of its _____ features. (origin)

2. Few employees are _____, and few want to work in the countryside. (loyally)

3. His words had a _____ effect on us. (magic)

4. Her face was _____ pale. (death)

5. To be a _____ man, you should try your best to study hard. (success)

6. The study is written from _____ experience. (person)

7. It was _____ whether the patient would survive the operation. (doubt)

8. Tom is charged with a theft and is now _____. (question)

9. We would be _____ if you could confirm your participation at your earliest convenience. (grate)

10. It's _____ to ask about a woman's age in some western countries. (offend)

Task 3

Directions: *Pay attention to different parts of speech and select the appropriate word to fill in the blanks.*

a. origin, original, originate, originally

1. April Fool's Day is widely observed now, but its _____ isn't certain.

Unit 5 Movie

2. Some soft wares are _____ invented for offices.

3. This article is full of _____ ideas.

4. Do you know where the Nile river _____?

b. die, dead, death

1. He was sentenced to _____.

2. Tom was shot _____ by a gunman outside his home.

3. The boy _____ for his beliefs.

c. produce, productive, producer

1. The drug _____ a feeling of excitement.

2. My time spent in the library was very _____.

3. Libya is a major oil _____.

d. real, really, realize, reality

1. The moment I saw her, I _____ something was wrong.

2. She is afraid of facing _____.

3. What I love about Internet is that it is _____ relaxing.

4. It wasn't a dream and it was a _____ person.

Task 4

Direction: *Rewrite the following sentences with the expressions in the box.*

| thanks to | for the time being | keep in mind | seem like |
| make sure | relate to | from a... perspective | offend |

1. I don't want to displease you.

_____

2. She's staying with her aunt at present.

_____

3. Try to see the issue in different ways.

4. Owning to your help, I finally passed the exam.

5. I'll remember your advice.

6. Remember to turn off the lights before you leave.

7. The lawyer read all the papers involving the case.

8. It seemed as a good idea.

Part Ⅳ   Reading Comprehension

Task 1

Directions: *Read the following passage and make the correct choice.*

The earliest intelligence test was designed to place children in appropriate school classes. At the beginning of the 20th century school authorities in Paris asked the psychologist Alfred Binet to design a method for picking out children who were unable to learn at a normal rate. Binet went on to develop a method that could measure the intelligence of every child—dull, bright, or normal. Binet realized that a person's ability to solve problems was an indication of intelligence. He found that complex problems, especially those involving abstract thinking, were best for distinguishing bright and dull students.

Problem-solving ability grows rapidly during childhood. Because of this, Binet decided to make an age scale of intelligence. He chose tasks for each age level that could be performed by most youngsters of that age but that could not be done by the

Unit 5 Movie

majority of children a year younger.

In 1905 Binet published a scale of intelligence for children from 3 to 13. Binet tests were adapted for American use in 1908. Since then many revisions of the Binet scales have been published in the United States and other countries.

1. What does this passage mainly discuss?

    A. Children's education.

    B. Children's intelligence.

    C. Intelligence tests.

    D. Children's ability

2. Alfred Binet was asked by school authorities in Paris to _____.

    A. find out a method to measure children's intelligence

    B. work out a way to tell dull children from normal ones

    C. determine children's ability to solve problems

    D. find the indications of intelligence in children

3. According to Binet, which of the following is the best to show the difference of intelligence?

    A. Problems involving hard work.

    B. Problems involving imagination.

    C. Problems involving ability.

    D. Problems involving abstract thinking.

4. The word "distinguishing" in Paragraph 1 (the last sentence) is closest in meaning to "_____".

    A. differing   B. marking

    C. excluding   D. combining

5. Today Binet intelligence tests have _____.

    A. been entirely accepted

    B. been totally rejected

    C. been considerably changed

    D. been firmly established

Task 2

Directions: *The following is a list of terms frequently used in films. After reading it, you are required to find the items equivalent to（与……等同）those given in Chinese in the table below.*

A — documentary writing
B — detective movie
C — movie star
D — stunt man
E — recording director
F — script girl
G — assistant director
H — film festival
I — Academy Awards(Oscar)
J — premiere
K — banned film
L — X-certificate
M — literary film
N — dubbed film
O — disaster film
P — western movie
Q — Universal Pictures Corporation

Example：电影明星(C)　　　　　电影节(H)
1. 特技替身演员(　)　　　　文艺片(　)
2. 首映式(　)　　　　　　　成人片(　)
3. 副导演(　)　　　　　　　西部片(　)
4. 禁映影片(　)　　　　　　录音师(　)
5. 译制片(　)　　　　　　　奥斯卡金像奖(　)

Task 3

Directions: *Complete the information by filling in the blanks. Write your answers in no more than 3 words.*

The trend towards globalization began seriously in the early 1970s when the system of fixed exchange rates was removed. This meant that the value of currencies would now be determined by the markets instead of individual governments. Other factors contributing to the rise of globalization are new communication technologies and better transportation systems. These have enabled companies to grow into

Unit 5 Movie

multinationals — producing goods on one side of the planet and selling them on the other.

But what is really holding globalization back is the lack of labor mobility（流动性）. Labor markets remain surprisingly national, even in areas like European Union, where citizens can live and work in any EU country. The main reasons for this are language and cultural barriers, recognized qualifications and, in some cases, strict immigration controls.

> This report is about (1) _____.
> Three factors that have contributed to globalization:
> removal of the system of (2) _____, new (3) _____ and better transportation systems.
> The lack of (4) _____ prevents globalization.
> One main reason for the very national labour markets is the barriers in (5) _____.

Task 4

Directions: *Complete the answers in no more than 3 words.*

Dear Sirs,

I am writing to confirm the loss of my credit card. I telephoned your office earlier today.

The details of my card are as follows. It is an Apex Silver card in the name of Paul Anderson. The credit card number is 5431 7602 2597 8431. I have had an Apex card since 1994. This card is valid from August 2003 to August 2005.

I lost the card yesterday at about 8:30 in the evening. The only case I used the card yesterday was to buy three dictionaries at the Dillons Bookstore in the Oxford Street. By accident, I left the card at the shop. When I realized what I had done, I telephoned the shop, but the shop assistants there could not find the card.

Could you please cancel my card immediately and make the necessary arrangements to issue a replacement card to me? I can be contacted at the telephone number of 347-4587-9056.

   Thank you for your assistance.

   Yours faithfully

   Paul Anderson

1. Why does the man write the letter?

   To _____ the loss of his credit card.

2. What's the name of the card?

   _____.

3. How long is the card valid?

   For _____ years.

4. Where did the man lose his card?

   At _____ in the Oxford Street.

5. What does the man ask the company to do about the lost card?

   He asks the company to issue _____ to him.

Part V   Translation

Directions: *This part is to test your ability to translate English into Chinese. Make the best choice and write the translation of the paragraph.*

1. After 10 years, millions of fans seem to have enjoyed the ride.

   A. 经过十年以后,成千上万的粉丝们会喜欢这个类型。

   B. 十年以后,许多粉丝们都热爱这种经历。

   C. 十年以后,数以百万的粉丝们似乎很享受这次体验。

2. There's no need to thank every single person you know.

   A. 你没必要感谢你认识的每一个人。

   B. 你不能感谢你认识的每一个人。

   C. 你没必要逐个感谢你认识的每一个人。

3. He didn't think it proper to tell his wife what had happened last night.
   A. 他不想把昨晚发生的事告诉妻子也不行。
   B. 他觉得还是不要把昨晚发生的事情告诉妻子为好。
   C. 他认为把昨晚发生的事情告诉他的妻子是不妥的。

4. He will come to call on you the moment he finishes his work.
   A. 他将去拜访你,只要他结束他工作。
   B. 他一做完他的工作就会去拜访你。
   C. 他一做完他的工作就会给你打电话来。

5. There were no less than 50 killed and wounded.
   A. 死伤者不少于五十人。
   B. 少于五十人死和伤。
   C. 死伤不超过五十个人。

6. Tomorrow morning could be more convenient, if it's all right with you.
   A. 如果你好了的话,明天上午更方便些。
   B. 如果你好了的话,明天上午会觉得更舒服些。
   C. 如果你觉得可以的话,明天上午更方便些。

Part Ⅵ Writing

Task 1

Directions: *Make up a complete sentence by joining the following words.*

1. friend, need, is, friend, a, indeed, in, a.

2. laughs, he, last, who, best, laughs.

3. limitless, youth, possibilities, means.

4. the, hot, is, iron, while, strike.

5. football, you, classroom, play, mustn't, in, the.

6. upwards, struggles, man, water, downwards, flows.

7. nowadays, popularity, studying, English, China, gains, in.

8. keeps, the, doctor, away, apple, an, day, a.

Task 2

Directions: *This part is to test your ability to do practical writing. You are required to write a note according to the information given below in Chinese.*

说明：假设你是陈涛(Chen Tao)，请以班长的名义按照下面的格式和内容给本班学生写一个内部通知。

主题：讨论班级规定

通知时间：2011年8月20日

内容：所有同学于8月22日晚7点在我班召开班会，讨论班级规定。任何人不得缺席。如有特殊情况不能参加者，请提前打电话给郭老师。如有任何问题，请联系陈涛。

Unit 6 Mother and Child

Part I Listening Comprehension

Task 1

Directions: *In this section you will hear 10 sentences. You are required to circle the word that you hear in brackets.*

1. Who is going to (wash/wish) it?
2. Would you like to (share/spare) it?
3. He (fetched/fished) it for me.
4. Do you know all the (words/worlds)?
5. Birds of a (feather/father) flock together.
6. You would better stay in the (zoo/room) for a day or two.
7. There are three (cocks/corks) over there.
8. Mary (shells/sells) peas.
9. I saw a red (bull/bowl).
10. That was a very good (goal/girl).

Task 2

Directions: *In this section you will hear one word from each of the following groups of words. Circle the one you hear.*

1. peak	tick	leak	lock	
2. bad	tag	gap	rap	
3. look	pooh	roof	soup	
4. vast	up	puff	rough	
5. floor	hot	god	oil	
6. peak	beat	cede	deal	
7. ago	hurt	per	serf	
8. lap	sip	dip	map	
9. at	eat	let	sit	
10. seed	head	board	add	

Task 3

Directions: *This section is to test your ability to give proper responses. There are 5 recorded questions in it. After each question, there is a pause. When you hear a question, you should decide on the correct answer from the 4 choices marked A, B, C and D.*

1. A. I don't like it. B. I go by bus.
   C. It's difficult. D. It's fine.

2. A. I'm playing football now. B. I'm going to play basketball.
   C. We'll meet at the gate. D. See you then.

3. A. Fine, I'd like. B. Yes, you may.
   C. I'm glad to. D. Well, just over there.

4. A. It's a famous city. B. Yes. I have come.
   C. I like it. D. Yes, it is.

5. A. See you. B. Just a moment, please.
   C. My pleasure. D. It's one o'clock.

Task 4

Directions: *This section is to test your ability to understand short dialogues. There are 5 recorded dialogues in it. After each dialogue, there is a recorded question. When you hear a question, you should decide on the correct*

answer from the 4 choices marked A, B, C and D.

1. A. Market. B. Going shopping.
   C. Supermarket D. The job fair.
2. A. Honest man. B. Friendly.
   C. Friendly and helpful. D. Very good.
3. A. 25 B. 65 C. 15 D. 40
4. A. It's going to rain. B. Ok. Fine.
   C. It has snowed. D. It begins to snow.
5. A. Where to have the meeting B. When to have the meeting
   C. Who to attend the meeting D. What to discuss at the meeting

Task 5

***Directions**: In this section, you will hear a short passage. There are five missing words or phrases in it. Fill in the blanks with the exact words or phrases you hear.*

There are four seasons in a year. They are spring, summer, autumn and winter. I like spring and autumn. The weather becomes (1) _____ gradually in spring. We can see flowers and hear the songs of the birds. The forests and the woods seem to be awakened and covered with (2) _____ color. In autumn the sky is blue and we feel (3) _____. The autumn is the (4) _____ time. The fruits are picked and the crops are (5) _____ in. We can eat fresh apples, bananas, peaches, oranges and grapes.

Part Ⅱ Dialogue

Task 1

***Directions**: Complete the following conversation by making the best choice in the table below.*

A: Hello, Liu Meimei!
B: Hello. Zhang Ming. Have you watched the news of CCTV?

A: Yes. (1)_____

B: That's too bad!

A: (2)_____

B: Yes, but I think it's more important to stop them from pouring water into our mother river.

A: (3)_____ But I don't know why they do so.

B: (4)_____ We'd better write a story about it to the TV station and the newspaper.

A: (5)_____ Businessmen are afraid of newspapers and TV stations.

A. Good idea.

B. Because they only think of money.

C. That's true.

D. I hope so.

E. Many fish have died in Changjiang River.

F. We have to take them to East Lake.

G. They built another paper factory by Changjiang River.

Task 2

Directions: *The following are some ways of making a request and responding to it. Read the words spoken and then match them with the functions.*

Words Spoken

A. I'd appreciate it very much if you could lend me your book.

B. No problem.

C. I was wondering if you could help me carry these boxes upstairs.

D. Would you mind opening the window? It's hot.

E. Can you pass me that pen?

F. No. I'm afraid I can't.

G. Mind your own business!

Unit 6 Mother and Child

H. This way, please.

I. Now, the floor is yours.

J. Get out of here.

Functions

1. You make a request asking someone to pass you the pen. _____

2. You try very politely to get someone to lend you a book. _____

3. You reject somebody's request directly but politely. _____

4. You make a tentative request because the task seems quite difficult. _____

5. You're glad to help and respond to someone's request positively and explicitly. _____

6. You tentatively request that someone open the window. _____

7. You rudely ask someone to attend to his own business. _____

8. You rudely order somebody to leave the room. _____

9. You politely request someone to follow you. _____

10. You make a ceremonial remark, requesting someone to make a speech. _____

Part Ⅲ Vocabulary & Structure

Task 1

Directions: *Complete each statement by choosing the appropriate answer from the 4 choices marked A, B, C and D.*

1. — That famous cherry trees _____ because of pollution.

   — Yes, we have to do something to save it.

   A. has died   B. had died   C. is dead   D. is dying

2. She ought to stop reading; she has a headache because she _____ too long.

   A. had read   B. read

C. is reading   D. has been reading

3. — You're talking too much.

    — Only at home. No one _____ me but you.

    A. is hearing   B. had heard

    C. heard   D. hears

4. — What have you been doing? I asked you a question. Why didn't you answer?

    — Sorry, I _____ to the news on the radio.

    A. listened   B. have listened

    C. was listening   D. had listened

5. — You should have told him the date earlier.

    — I _____, but he forgot about it.

    A. did   B. have   C. had   D. should have

6. — Tom's wife took the place of him to attend the conference.

    — I would rather Tom _____ there, not his wife.

    A. had been   B. have been

    C. was   D. went

7. — Listen!

    — I _____ but I _____ anything at all.

    A. listened; have heard   B. have listened; hear

    C. was listening; wasn't hearing D. am listening; don't hear

8. The shop assistant promised me that the material _____ and what she said _____ to be true.

    A. would be dried easily; was proved   B. will be dried easily; was proved

    C. dried easily; proved   D. was dried easily; proved

9. A friendly basketball match between teachers and students _____ tomorrow afternoon. Anybody is welcome.

    A. was held   B. is held

    C. must be held   D. will be held

10. — Did you see Marty in the manager's office?

    — Yes, he _____ by the manager.

Unit 6 Mother and Child

   A. is questioned   B. was being questioned

   C. had been questioned   D. was questioned

11. — Who will go to the airport to meet Jenny?

    — I will. I _____ her several times. I can find her easily.

    A. met   B. have met

    C. had met   D. will meet

12. — I've not finished my project yet.

    — Hurry up! Our friends _____ for us.

    A. are waiting   B. wait   C. will wait   D. have waited

13. — He's never stolen anything before, _____ he?

    — _____. It's his second time to be taken to the police station.

    A. has, Yes   B. is, Yes

    C. hasn't, Yes   D. has, No

14. — How did you _____ your summer holidays this year?

    — Reading and surfing.

    A. take   B. use   C. spend   D. enjoy

15. — People find it hard to get across the river.

    — I think at least two bridges _____ over it.

    A. need   B. are needing

    C. will need   D. are needed

Task 2

Directions: *There are 10 incomplete statements here. You should fill each blank with the proper form of the word given in brackets.*

1. We can't judge a person by _____. (appear)

2. TV provides universal _____ (entertain)

3. Would you like to make a _____ to our charity appeal? (donate)

4. In case of _____, press the alarm button. (emerge)

5. I don't know how to _____ (express) my thanks.

6. Although they all come from Britain, they speak English _____. (different)

7. You are not _____ (allow) to smoke here.

8. What were his _____ (actually) words?

9. Do you know what American _____ (educate) is focused on?

10. _____ is crucial to a business' fame. (honest)

Task 3

Directions: *Pay attention to different parts of speech and select the appropriate word to fill in the blanks.*

a. decide, decision, decisive

1. I don't want to make any wrong _____ and regret later.

2. It was the _____ battle of the entire war.

3. Think about it very carefully before you _____.

b. considerate, consideration, considering

1. Time is another important _____.

2. She's very active, _____ his age.

3. It was very _____ of him to wait.

c. agree, disagree, agreement

1. Jane has _____ to attend the party with us tomorrow evening.

2. They finally reach an _____ that all should make efforts to keep this area peaceful.

3. We _____ with him since he could not offer convincing reasons.

d. emerge, emergence, emergency

1. Our plane had an engine problem and had to perform an _____ landing.

2. After weeks of rain, the sun finally _____ from behind the clouds.

3. The last few years have seen the _____ of some undesirable phenomena in this area.

Unit 6 Mother and Child

e. diplomacy, diplomat, diplomatic

1. To be a _____, he should master many kinds of language.
2. _____ is better than war.
3. He will go far in the _____ service.

Task 4

Direction: *Rewrite the following sentences with the expressions in the box.*

| up to par | actually | pass through | blossom into |
| deal with | blurt out | raise | cool down |

1. He experienced a difficult period shortly after his marriage broke down.

2. He has grown into a man.

3. He said the truth suddenly without thinking carefully enough.

4. You should know how to solve this problem.

5. The TV programme is not as good as usual.

6. We want to bring up our children to be outstanding talent.

7. When you meet something in trouble, firstly you must calm down.

8. She looks young, but in fact she's 50.

Part Ⅳ   Reading Comprehension

Task 1

Directions: *Read the following passage and make the correct choice.*

Do you find getting up in the morning so difficult that it's painful? This might be called laziness, but Dr. Kleitman has a new explanation. He has proved that everyone has a daily energy cycle.

During the hours when you labour through your work you may say that you're "hot". That's true. The time of day when you feel most energetic is when your cycle of body temperature is at its peak. For some people the peak comes during the forenoon. For other it comes in the afternoon or evening. No one has discovered why this is so, but it leads to such familiar monologues (自言自语) as: Get up, John! You'll be late for work again! The possible explanation to the trouble is that John is at his temperature and energy peak in the evening. Much family quarrelling ends when husbands and wives realize what this energy means, and which cycle each member of the family has.

You can't change your energy cycle, but you can learn to make your life fit it better. Habit can help, Dr. Kleitman believes. Maybe you're sleepy in the evening but feel you must stay up late anyway. Counteract your cycle to some extent by habitually staying up late than you want to. If your energy is low in the morning but you have an important job to do early in the day, rise before your usual hour. This won't change your cycle, but you'll get steam and work better at your low point.

Get off to a slow start which saves your energy. Get up with a leisurely yawn and stretch. Sit on the edge of the bed a minute before putting your feet on the floor. Avoid the troublesome search for clean clothes by laying them out at night before. Whenever possible, do routine work in the afternoon and save tasks requiring more energy of concentration for your sharper hours.

1. What is discussed in this passage?

   A. Man's energy cycle and how to fit it.   B. An explanation to late rising.

Unit 6 Mother and Child

C. Suggestions to late risers.   D. How to change your habits.

2. According to his passage, the time when you say you are "hot" is the time _____.

   A. when your body temperature is near the highest point

   B. when you feel most energetic

   C. when you catch a fever

   D. when you labour through your work during the forenoon

3. It is very likely that a person who has trouble in getting up early is _____.

   A. a person without a daily energy cycle

   B. a lazy person

   C. most vigorous in the afternoon or evening

   D. a person who can't reach his temperature-and-energy peak

4. The author advises that to keep our energy or work, we should _____.

   A. get out of bed immediately when we are awake

   B. do some morning exercises

   C. get clean clothes ready for next day's use before going to bed

   D. go to bed earlier than usual

5. What is FALSE according to this passage?

   A. Family quarrels may result from the unawareness of the energy cycles of family members.

   B. We can change our energy cycles by changing our habits.

   C. Even Dr. Kleitman can not provide a satisfactory answer to the question why people reach their peaks at different hours of a day.

   D. To a person whose energy is low in the morning, it is advisable for him to rise earlier than usual so as to work more efficiently at his low point.

Task 2

***Directions**: The following is a list of terms frequently used in daily family life. After reading it, you are required to find the items equivalent to (与……等同) those given in Chinese in the table below.*

A — mothers love
B — Thanksgiving education
C — family ties
D — photo album
E — family tree
F — relatives
G — harmonious society
H — family party
I — flesh and blood
J — companionship family
K — brotherly affection
L — husband and wife treating each other with courtesy
M — true love
N — national wealth and benefits to descendants
O — Chicken soup for the soul
P — enjoy the love of family
Q — bring honour to one's ancestors

Example：相册（D）　　　　　　真爱（M）
1. 感恩教育（　）　　　　　母爱（　）
2. 骨肉亲情（　）　　　　　手足情深（　）
3. 心灵鸡汤（　）　　　　　国富民强（　）
4. 天伦之乐（　）　　　　　光宗耀祖（　）
5. 家谱（　）　　　　　　　家庭聚会（　）

Task 3

Directions: *Complete the information by filling in the blanks. Write your answers in no more than 3 words.*

Dear Dr. Yamata,

　　The Association of Asian Economic Studies is pleased to invite you to be this year's guest speaker at its annual international symposium（讨论会）. The symposium will be held for 3 days from December 22nd to 24th, 2011. This year's topic will be Economic Development in Asia. About 100 people from various countries will be attending the symposium. They would be pleased to meet you and share their views with you.

　　The Association will cover all the expenses of your trip to this symposium.

Unit 6 Mother and Child

As the program is to be announced on December 1st, 2011, will you kindly let us know before that time whether your busy schedule will allow you to attend our symposium? We are looking forward to your favorable reply.

Yours sincerely,
John Smith
Secretary of Association of Asian Economic Studies

> Writer of the letter: (1) _____
> Organizer of the Symposium: Association of (2) _____
> Guest speaker to be invited: Dr. Yamata
> Starting date of the symposium: (3) _____
> Number of guests invited: (4) _____
> Topic of the symposium: (5) _____ in Asia

Task 4

Directions: *Complete the answers in no more than 3 words.*

Hundreds of years ago, a Roman army came north from England to make war on Scotland. The Scots fought hard to drive the enemy out of Scotland, but there were too many of the Romans. It looked as if the Romans would win.

One night, the leader of the Scots marched his soldiers to the top of a hill. "We will rest here tonight, my men." He said, "Tomorrow we will fight one more battle. We must win, or we will die." They were all very tired. So they ate their supper quickly and fell asleep. There were four guards on duty, but they were too tired, and one by one they fell asleep.

The Romans were not asleep. Quickly they gathered at the foot of the hill and came up near the Scots. Suddenly, one of them put his foot on a thistle. He cried out and his sudden cry woke the Scots. In a minute, they were on their feet and ready for a battle. The fighting was hard, but it did not last long. The Scots wiped out the Romans and saved Scotland.

The thistle is not a beautiful plant. It has sharp needles all over it. Few people liked it. But the people of Scotland liked it so much that they made it their national flower.

1. On which country did the Romans make war?
   _____.

2. How was the situation at the beginning of the war?
   It was in the favour of _____.

3. How did the Scots fight against the Romans?
   They fought _____.

4. Why did the Roman soldier cry when the Romans tried to make a sudden attack on the Scots?
   Because his foot was hurt by _____.

5. What was the result of the war?
   The Romans were _____.

Part Ⅴ   Translation

Directions: *This part is to test your ability to translate English into Chinese. Make the best choice and write the translation of the paragraph.*

1. My mother insisted upon knowing where we were at all times.
   A. 我妈妈总是打探我们的行踪。
   B. 我妈妈主张了解我们的行踪。
   C. 我妈妈主张我们一直在原来的地方。

2. Time proved that the baby's hearing was perfect.
   A. 时间证明孩子的听力是完全没有问题的。
   B. 时间是能证明一切的,孩子的听力是可以的。
   C. 一切都已时间为准,都要关注孩子的听力。

Unit 6 Mother and Child

3. Mother said she was glad she never let her hair be cut.
   A. 妈妈说她很高兴从没有剪过头发。
   B. 妈妈真高兴,她不会剪头发。
   C. 妈妈说她高兴是因为想剪头发。

4. Really good cooks are few and far between.
   A. 真正好的厨师不多,他们之间的关系疏远。
   B. 真正好的厨师不多。
   C. 真正好的厨师之间的竞争是激烈的。

5. But for the help and encouragement of my friends, I would have never won this prize.
   A. 要不是朋友的帮助和鼓励,我永远也不可能赢得这个奖项。
   B. 但是为了朋友的帮助和鼓励,我永远也不可能赢得这个奖项。
   C. 要不是朋友的帮助和鼓励,我应该早就获得这个奖项了。

6. Given that she is interested in music, I am sure composition is the right career for her.
   A. 鉴于她喜欢音乐,我能确信她把作曲视为终生的职业。
   B. 如果她喜欢音乐,我相信她的职业就只能是作曲。
   C. 鉴于她喜欢音乐,我相信作曲对于她来说是一个合适的职业。

Part Ⅵ Writing

Task 1

Directions: *Make up a complete sentence by joining the following words.*

1. out, sight, of, out, mind, of.

2. friend, my, best, other, is, from, my, different, friends.

3. time, precious, is, so, that, can't, afford, to, waste, we, it.

4. Rome, not, in, built, day, a, was.

5. should, we, habit, get, into, the, of, good, hours, keeping.

6. had, I, meanest, in, the, mother, whole, world, the.

7. it, that, is, conceivable, knowledge, role, plays, important, in, our, an, life.

8. mother, glad, never, she, let, hair, her, cut, be, said, was, she.

Task 2

Directions: *This part is to test your ability to do practical writing. You are required to write a business letter according to the following instructions given in Chinese.*

说明：假定你是销售部经理王明，根据下列信息写一封信。
写信日期：2011年6月19日
收信人：Mr. John Brown
内容：1. 感谢对方订购了你公司的最新产品；
2. 所订购的货物已发出，大约一周后到达；
3. 收到货物后请回复；
4. 希望能继续与对方合作。

答案及听力材料

Key to Unit 1

Part Ⅰ Listening Comprehension

Task 1

1. boat 2. fill 3. pen 4. hope 5. leave 6. time
7. down 8. hat 9. key 10. gets

Task 2

1. service 2. life 3. way 4. sip 5. zip 6. tongue
7. park 8. late 9. soil 10. ship

Task 3

1. A 2. D 3. A 4. B 5. A

Task 4

1. B 2. A 3. C 4. C 5. B

Task 5

1. friendly 2. own 3. hurt 4. noise 5. habits

Part Ⅱ Dialogue

Task 1

1. A 2. C 3. G 4. D 5. B

Task 2

1. A 2. B 3. E 4. C 5. D 6. I 7. G 8. H 9. F

Part Ⅲ Vocabulary & Structure

Task 1

1. B 2. D 3. C 4. B 5. C 6. A 7. B 8. D 9. A
10. C 11. B 12. C 13. C 14. C 15. A

Task 2

1. are involved 2. is included 3. practical 4. regardless 5. highlight
6. to maintain 7. positively 8. splendid 9. financial 10. majority

Task 3

a. confidently; confidence; confident

b. add; additional; addition

c. practice; impractical; practical

d. recommend; recommendation; recommended

e. adequately; adequate; inadequate

Task 4

1. The sales man finds it easy to take in old ladies.

2. I went out regardless of the rain.

3. If you were in the Sahara, you would be aware of the value of fresh water.

4. Nothing would tempt me to live here.

5. The English alphabet starts with A.

6. His remarks highlighted his own function.

7. Her family's support is particularly precious to Mary.

8. Her eyes took a while to accommodate to the darkness.

Part Ⅳ Reading Comprehension

Task 1

1. C 2. B 3. B 4. D 5. C

Task 2

1. D E 2. K L 3. O J 4. P Q 5. A M

答案及听力材料

Task 3

(1) beautiful weather (2) wonderful scenery (3) 71.9℉

(4) 23 inches (5) warm sunshine

Task 4

1. a travel agency 2. 7:00 a.m. 3. Temple of Heaven

4. 3:45 p.m. 5. jackets or ties

Part V Translation

1. A 2. C 3. C 4. A 5. B 6. A

Part VI Writing

Task 1

1. Mary has got yellow hair.

2. I like watching TV very much.

3. Let's do exercises every day!

4. What shall we do this evening?

5. Experience is the mother of wisdom.

6. College life has given us a new experience.

7. I'm looking forward to your coming to Shanghai.

8. Here is the first suggestion for freshmen.

Task 2

> Shicheng Electronics Ltd.
>
> Chen Yang
>
> Electronics Engineer
>
> Address: No. 36 Minjiang Road, Chaoyang District
>
> E-mail: cy1978@163.com
>
> Tel: 010-87652100
>
> Mobilephone: 13855623234

Script for Listening Comprehension

Part Ⅰ Listening Comprehension

Task 1

Directions: In this section you will hear 10 sentences. You are required to circle the word that you hear in brackets.

1. The (boat/bought) is very small.
2. I want you to (feel/fill) this dish.
3. The old man's (pan/pen) leaks.
4. I (hope/help) that you will have a good time.
5. Is he going to (leave/live)?
6. This (time/tame) he needs to have a lunch with your family.
7. Please sit (done/down).
8. Li Ming's (hat/hate) is very beautiful.
9. At length the young girl found her (key/king) to the lab.
10. At last, the boy (gates/gets) to the bus station.

Task 2

Directions: In this section you will hear one word from each of the following groups of words. Circle the one you hear.

1. service 2. life 3. way 4. sip 5. zip 6. tongue
7. park 8. late 9. soil 10. ship

Task 3

Directions: This section is to test your ability to give proper responses. There are 5 recorded questions in it. After each question, there is a pause. When you hear a question, you should decide on the correct answer from the 4 choices marked A, B, C and D.

1. Who is this? Can you guess?
2. How do you do?
3. Where are you from?
4. Li Hua, do you know the time?

答案及听力材料

5. Is everyone here today, Zhang Hong?

Task 4

Directions: *This section is to test your ability to understand short dialogues. There are 5 recorded dialogues in it. After each dialogue, there is a recorded question. When you hear a question, you should decide on the correct answer from the 4 choices marked A, B, C and D.*

1. W: What's the date today?
   M: March the 8th.
   Q: What's the woman asking?

2. M: What time do we have to check in then?
   W: Around 3:20.
   Q: What's the man asking about?

3. M: What can I do for you?
   W: I'd like to buy a jacket.
   Q: Where are they?

4. W: These caps look nice. How much is each?
   M: Ten dollars each.
   Q: How much will the woman pay if she buys one?

5. M: I'd like to buy a bike for my son.
   W: What colour does he prefer?
   Q: What's the man doing?

Task 5

Directions: *In this section, you will hear a short passage. There are five missing words or phrases in it. Fill in the blanks with the exact words or phrases you hear.*

These are the things we learn. No matter how old you are, share everything. Don't hit people and play <u>friendly</u>. Keep your <u>own</u> room clean and put things back where you found them. Don't take things that aren't yours. Wash your hands before you eat. When you <u>hurt</u> somebody, you must say you're sorry. Don't make <u>noise</u> when someone is studying or sleeping. Get into good <u>habits</u>. Get up early and never be late for school or work. Go to bed on time. Always remember to learn.

Key to Unit 2

Part Ⅰ Listening Comprehension

Task 1

1. books 2. Pull 3. long 4. walk 5. afraid 6. bird
7. fast 8. left 9. eyes 10. knocked

Task 2

1. dick 2. gab 3. bail 4. tale 5. muck 6. took
7. could 8. turn 9. foot 10. lot

Task 3

1. D 2. C 3. A 4. B 5. A

Task 4

1. D 2. B 3. D 4. C 5. A

Task 5

1. First 2. trade 3. written 4. travel 5. communicate

Part Ⅱ Dialogue

Task 1

1. D 2. A 3. E 4. C 5. G

Task 2

1. B 2. C 3. D 4. A 5. H 6. F 7. E 8. I 9. G 10. J

Part Ⅲ Vocabulary & Structure

Task 1

1. C 2. A 3. B 4. C 5. C 6. A 7. B 8. C 9. A 10. C

Task 2

1. description 2. abnormal 3. imitating 4. musical 5. practice
6. efforts 7. to take 8. received 9. talented 10. continuous

答案及听力材料

Task 3

    a. succeed; successful; success

    b. relate; relatives; relation

    c. magical; magic; magician

    d. wondering; wonderful; wonder

    e. invented; inventor; invention

Task 4

1. Who'd like to describe what happened just now?

2. A reply came promptly.

3. I have been crazy about him since the first time I saw him.

4. It turns out that with a tiny rewrite this can be achieved.

5. It was nothing less than a disaster.

6. She continues to practice these skills in her classroom every day.

7. I must ask you to accompany me to the police station.

8. The boy's unusual behaviour puzzled the doctor.

Part Ⅳ Reading Comprehension

Task 1

1. A 2. D 3. B 4. D 5. A

Task 2

1. N O 2. A Q 3. C D 4. H E 5. L P

Task 3

(1) Safe to mail   (2) lost or stolen   (3) Good records

(4) Refuse to pay   (5) an overdraft fee

Task 4

1. looking after children   2. English and French   3. uninteresting

4. less important   4. a gardener

Part Ⅴ Translation

1. A 2. C 3. B 4. C 5. C 6. B

Part Ⅵ Writing

Task 1

1. Have you written a diary?

2. We would like to go by bike.

3. Seeing is believing.

4. God helps those who helps themselves.

5. Well begun is half done.

6. Such music must come from heaven.

7. We should do our best to achieve our goal in life.

8. The more books we read, the more learned we become.

Task 2

> Dear Xiao Yun,
>
>   Congratulations on moving into the new flat. I bought this vase. I think you will like it. So I take this opportunity to give it to you as a small gift, in the hope that it will give more decoration to your beautiful new house.
>
>   Best wishes to you for a happy life in the new house.
>
>   Yours lovely,
>
>   Xiao Qian

Script for Listening Comprehension

Part Ⅰ Listening Comprehension

Task 1

Directions: *In this section you will hear 10 sentences. You are required to circle the word that you hear in brackets.*

1. Jim had two (bucks/<u>books</u>).

2. The sign on the door said: (Poor/<u>Pull</u>).

答案及听力材料

3. The blue pen looks very (long/lung).
4. In the evening, we should (walk/work) a while.
5. I am (afraid/Africa) not to complete this task.
6. We caught a (beard/bird).
7. We should eat a little (fast/vast) food.
8. Jane (left/leaf) this school two years ago.
9. The little girl's (eyes/ice) are very beautiful.
10. No sooner had I (knack/knocked) than she opened the door.

Task 2

Directions: *In this section you will hear one word from each of the following groups of words. Circle the one you hear.*

1. dick   2. gab   3. bail   4. tale   5. muck   6. took
7. could   8. turn   9. foot   10. lot

Task 3

Directions: *This section is to test your ability to give proper responses. There are 5 recorded questions in it. After each question, there is a pause. When you hear a question, you should decide on the correct answer from the 4 choices marked A, B, C and D.*

1. Do you often read the newspapers?
2. Can I use your dictionary?
3. What day is it today?
4. What's that under the desk?
5. Whose white dog is this?

Task 4

Directions: *This section is to test your ability to understand short dialogues. There are 5 recorded dialogues in it. After each dialogue, there is a recorded question. When you hear a question, you should decide on the correct answer from the 4 choices marked A, B, C and D.*

1. W: Excuse me, would you mind if I use your pen?
   M: Not at all. It's over there on the desk.
   Q: What does she want to do?

103

2. W: What kind of room do you want to book, sir?

   M: I'd like to book a single room.

   Q: What's the man doing?

3. W: I'm going to the station. Can you drive me there?

   M: Yes. It's my pleasure.

   Q: What does she ask the man to do?

4. M: Why don't you try to finish your homework? I'll cook you the supper.

   W: I'd rather make it by myself.

   Q: What can we learn about the woman?

5. M: What did you have?

   W: We had roast beef and potatoes.

   Q: What does the man ask?

Task 5

Directions: *In this section, you will hear a short passage. There are five missing words or phrases in it. Fill in the blanks with the exact words or phrases you hear.*

Why do all these people want to learn English? Why do we learn English? <u>First</u> of all, English is one of the world's most widely used languages. It is the international language of <u>trade</u>. It is the language of Britain, the USA, Australia, Canada and so on. Secondly, most books and newspapers are <u>written</u> in English. We want to learn high technology from other countries. Thirdly, we want to <u>travel</u> to other countries, and you can make friends with those who like English and make your life much more colorful. With the help of English, we can <u>communicate</u> with people of many countries.

Key to Unit 3

Part I Listening Comprehension

Task 1

1. bus 2. glass 3. save 4. bike 5. boy 6. ringing

7. garage 8. mouth 9. Though 10. known

答案及听力材料

Task 2

1. pressure 2. breeze 3. fourth 4. hate 5. hurt

6. ago 7. sip 8. seed 9. peak 10. gap

Task 3

1. C 2. A 3. D 4. A 5. D

Task 4

1. B 2. D 3. C 4. C 5. A

Task 5

1. rich 2. forests 3. exports 4. mineral 5. electricity

Part Ⅱ Dialogue

Task 1

1. C 2. F 3. D 4. G 5. J 6. E 7. I 8. A 9. H 10. B

Task 2

1. H 2. I 3. B 4. J 5. G 6. C 7. A 8. E 9. D 10. F

Part Ⅲ Vocabulary & Structure

Task 1

1. D 2. D 3. A 4. B 5. C 6. C 7. D 8. B 9. A

10. C 11. D 12. A 13. D 14. C 15. D

Task 2

1. competitiveness 2. externally 3. amazingly 4. pride 5. civic

6. spectacle 7. celebrities 8. expect 9. requirements 10. skillful/skilled

Task 3

a. comfortably; comfortable; comfort

b. opposite; oppose; opposing

c. unexpected; expect; expectation

d. celebrity; celebrities; celebrate

e. compete; competitors; competitive

Task 4

1. He has got loads of money.

105

2. All of a sudden, I remembered that I hadn't locked the door.

3. Children should look up to their parents.

4. We are proud of offering the best service in town.

5. They came to the baseball field to root for their school team.

6. There is a wedding going on at the church.

7. We shall dress the hall up for the National Day.

8. Tune in to BBC tonight at 9 o'clock.

Part Ⅳ   Reading Comprehension

Task 1

1. B   2. A   3. C   4. A   5. D

Task 2

1. B   H   2. K   P   3. O   Q   4. F   M   5. A   N

Task 3

1. an agenda   2. in advance   3. speed up

4. the topics   5. the meeting's function

Task 4

1. the sales department   2. from abroad   3. Spanish and Italian

4. 21   5. Washington State

Part Ⅴ   Translation

1. A   2. A   3. B   4. C   5. C   6. C

Part Ⅵ   Writing

Task 1

1. It is a revolutionary invention.

2. Overwork does harm to health.

3. Reading does good to our mind.

4. The Super Bowl is the biggest football game of the year.

5. I haven't seen you since we graduated.

6. Smoking has a great influence on our health.

7. Gold medals will be given to the best athletes.

8. The biggest football game of the year brings high expectations.

Task 2

> **Lost and Found**
> A man has picked a wrist watch in the shopping center and turned it over to our office. The owner of the wrist watch may come to claim it with his or her identification card.
> Lost and Found Office

Script for Listening Comprehension

Part I Listening Comprehension

Task 1

Directions: *In this section you will hear 10 sentences. You are required to circle the word that you hear in brackets.*

1. Look! This (bus/bath) is coming.

2. This (glass/glas) is very cool.

3. Lily said, "We should (sieve/save) time."

4. The (bike/bake) is Jane's.

5. That (boil/boy) looks very handsome.

6. The bell is (ringing/running).

7. Tom's (garage/Gareth) is very large.

8. Please open your (month/mouth) and say "a".

9. (Though/Through) he is great, he must go away.

10. As is (no, known) to the world, China has achieved an economic miracle.

Task 2

Directions: *In this section you will hear one word from each of the following groups of words. Circle the one you hear.*

1. pressure 2. breeze 3. fourth 4. hate 5. hurt 6. ago

7. sip 8. seed 9. peak 10. gap

Task 3

Directions**:** *This section is to test your ability to give proper responses. There are 5 recorded questions in it. After each question, there is a pause. When you hear a question, you should decide on the correct answer from the 4 choices marked A, B, C and D.*

1. Which do you prefer, coffee or tea?

2. Would you like to come to the party?

3. Where is the nearest hotel?

4. How do you like the book?

5. Why are you late for work?

Task 4

Directions**:** *This section is to test your ability to understand short dialogues. There are 5 recorded dialogues in it. After each dialogue, there is a recorded question. When you hear a question, you should decide on the correct answer from the 4 choices marked A, B, C and D.*

1. M: Could you tell me how to get to the library, please?

   W: Yes. Go along this road to the second cross road.

   Q: What's the man doing?

2. W: Hello, may I speak to Mr. Smith?

   M: Sorry he's out.

   Q: What does the woman want to do?

3. M: Where shall we go for dinner?

   W: I... I want to lose some weight.

   Q: What does the woman mean?

4. M: Where shall we meet?

   W: How about the school gate?

   Q: Where will they meet?

5. M: Would you like to go out?

   W: Sorry, I can't. I have to finish a report.

   Q: What's the woman doing?

答案及听力材料

Task 5

Directions: *In this section, you will hear a short passage. There are five missing words or phrases in it. Fill in the blanks with the exact words or phrases you hear.*

Canada is a large country. To the west of it is the Pacific Ocean. To the east is the Atlantic Ocean. Canada is a very <u>rich</u> country. It is rich in forests, fish, minerals and so on. It is <u>forests</u> that spread across the country. Most of the tress are evergreen trees. Canada <u>exports</u> more fish than any other country in the world. There are some very important <u>mineral</u> ores(矿物)in the country. They are iron ore, gold and silver, and coal and oil. Canada has many lakes and rivers. It is easy to make <u>electricity</u> from the water.

Key to Unit 4

Part Ⅰ Listening Comprehension

Task 1

1. year's   2. fair   3. cure   4. close   5. sound   6. rules
7. tree   8. Drop   9. doctor   10. watch

Task 2

1. tear   2. fair   3. sure   4. most   5. found   6. wrap
7. try   8. chap   9. cage   10. weak

Task 3

1. C   2. A   3. D   4. B   5. B

Task 4

1. A   2. C   3. D   4. B   5. A

Task 5

1. better   2. parking   3. petrol   4. enjoying   5. unpleasant

Part Ⅱ Dialogue

Task 1

1. C   2. F   3. A   4. E   5. D

Task 2

1. G 2. J 3. C 4. E 5. I 6. H 7. D 8. B 9. A 10. F

Part Ⅲ Vocabulary & Structure

Task 1

1. C 2. B 3. A 4. A 5. D 6. D 7. A 8. C 9. C
10. B 11. D 12. B 13. A 14. B 15. B

Task 2

1. historical 2. inspiring 3. romantic 4. adjust 5. disconnected
6. specially 7. creativity 8. preserved 9. depends 10. failure

Task 3

a. likely; alike; like

b. created; creative; creation

c. traditional; Traditionally; tradition

d. preserver; preserve; preserved

e. Unable; able; capable

Task 4

1. The government has set out to make many needed reforms.

2. Because of your help, we were successful.

3. Snails are considered a delicacy in France.

4. He speaks not only English but also Japanese.

5. If you do decide to use it, what would you do with it?

6. She insisted on leaving at once.

7. The book is superior to that.

8. I look forward to hearing from you.

Part Ⅳ Reading Comprehension

Task 1

1. C 2. D 3. A 4. D 5. C

Task 2

1. Q N 2. J O 3. K L 4. M D 5. G E

答案及听力材料

Task 3

1. Brain Store   2. two business days   3. phone   4. fax   5. 90 days

Task 4

1. buying or subscribing   2. word of mouth   3. Advertising

4. reach every home   5. still make profit

Part Ⅴ   Translation

1. A   2. C   3. C   4. C   5. B   6. A

Part Ⅵ   Writing

Task 1

1. The job requires great patience.

2. That's the reason why I don't like it.

3. The computer is a wonderful machine.

4. Listening to music enables us to feel relaxed.

5. Is there any fish on the menu?

6. A journey of a thousand miles begins with a single step.

7. Actions speak louder than words.

8. Do what you say, say what you do.

Task 2

> Dear Dean Fang,
>
>   I'm having a bad cold these days, so I'd like to apply for a two-day leave of absence from May 26th to May 27th in order to see the doctor.
>
>   I would be grateful if you grant me my application. As to the lessons during my absence, I will try my best to make them up as soon as possible.
>
> Yours sincerely,
Xiao Liang

Script for Listening Comprehension

Part Ⅰ Listening Comprehension

Task 1

Directions: *In this section you will hear 10 sentences. You are required to circle the word that you hear in brackets.*

1. A (<u>year's</u>/ear's) plan start with spring.
2. All is (fare/<u>fair</u>) in war.
3. Prevention is better than the (<u>cure</u>/curl).
4. A (cloth/<u>close</u>) mouth catches no flies.
5. A (<u>sound</u>/sun) ruined is in a sound body.
6. Reason (<u>rules</u>/roles) all things.
7. As the (<u>tree</u>/train), so the fruit.
8. (Draw/<u>Drop</u>) water with a sieve.
9. Has the (daughter/<u>doctor</u>) arrived?
10. Harm (<u>watch</u>/wash), harm catch.

Task 2

Directions: *In this section you will hear one word from each of the following groups of words. Circle the one you hear.*

1. tear   2. fair   3. sure   4. most   5. found   6. wrap

7. try   8. chap   9. cage   10. weak

Task 3

Directions: *This section is to test your ability to give proper responses. There are 5 recorded questions in it. After each question, there is a pause. When you hear a question, you should decide on the correct answer from the 4 choices marked A, B, C and D.*

1. How are you getting along?
2. When will the meeting begin?
3. Would you mind turning down the TV?
4. What's wrong with you?

5. What can I do for you?

Task 4

Directions: *This section is to test your ability to understand short dialogues. There are 5 recorded dialogues in it. After each dialogue, there is a recorded question. When you hear a question, you should decide on the correct answer from the 4 choices marked A, B, C and D.*

1. W: Will you be free this evening? Would you like to go dancing this evening?
   M: Ok. That's a good idea.
   Q: What does the man mean?

2. M: Li Hong, you look so bad. What's the matter?
   W: It's the English exam
   Q: What's the matter with the woman?

3. W: Good afternoon. Welcome to our restaurant.
   M: Good afternoon
   Q: What does the man want to do?

4. M: It's just ten o'clock. Can't you stay a little longer?
   W: I'm afraid I must go now. I have an appointment with Mr. Hopkins at ten thirty.
   Q: When will the woman meet Mr. Hopkins?

5. W: Right! I like listening to all kinds of music.
   M: Well. Whose music do you like best?
   Q: What does the woman like?

Task 5

Directions: *In this section, you will hear a short passage. There are five missing words or phrases in it. Fill in the blanks with the exact words or phrases you hear.*

I like to use my bicycle for short journeys. It is <u>better</u> than waiting for a bus. On my bike I can get a lot of exercises and fresh air, and this can make me happy and feel younger.

If you live in a big city, it is often faster than a car. You can leave your bike anywhere, so you needn't worry about <u>parking</u>. The bike needn't use <u>petrol</u>, gas or any other fuel. So we have been <u>enjoying</u> the benefits of cycling for years. So bikes are good for our city or town, do you think so?

I use it most in summer, autumn, spring when the weather is warm and dry. Of course it can be <u>unpleasant</u> in winter, for it is cold and often the rain is heavy.

Key to Unit 5

Part Ⅰ Listening Comprehension

Task 1

1. cop   2. wit   3. Years   4. meet   5. Learn   6. its

7. saying   8. threw   9. one   10. right

Task 2

1. word   2. unit   3. beam   4. fine   5. down   6. boats

7. roads   8. lord   9. mouse   10. slow

Task 3

1. C   2. A   3. B   4. C   5. A

Task 4

1. C   2. C   3. D   4. C   5. A

Task 5

1. experience   2. buy   3. based   4. spend   5. patience

Part Ⅱ Dialogue

Task 1

1. F   2. E   3. H   4. B   5. I   6. D   7. A   8. C   9. G   10. J

Task 2

1. G   2. C   3. B   4. D   5. F   6. H   7. E   8. I   9. A

Part Ⅲ Vocabulary & Structure

Task 1

1. C   2. A   3. C   4. B   5. D   6. B   7. D   8. D   9. B

10. D   11. C   12. B   13. B   14. C   15. D

答案及听力材料

Task 2

1. original 2. loyal 3. magic 4. deathly 5. successful 6. personal

7. doubtly 8. being questioned 9. grateful 10. offensive

Task 3

a. origin; originally; original; originates

b. death; dead; died

c. produces; productive; producers

d. realized; reality; really; real

Task 4

1. I don't want to offend you.

2. She's staying with her aunt for the time being.

3. Try to see the issue from a different perspective.

4. Thanks to your help, I finally passed the exam.

5. I'll keep your advice in mind.

6. Make sure to turn off the lights before you leave.

7. The lawyer read all the papers relating to the case.

8. It seemed like a good idea.

Part IV Reading Comprehension

Task 1

1. C 2. B 3. D 4. A 5. C

Task 2

1. D M 2. J L 3. G P 4. K E 5. N I

Task 3

1. globalization 2. fixed exchange rates 3. communication technologies

4. labor mobility 5. language and culture

Task 4

1. confirm 2. Apex silver 3. two

4. the Dillons Bookstore 5. a replacement card

Part V Translation

1. C 2. A 3. C 4. B 5. A 6. C

Part VI Writing

Task 1

1. A friend in need is a friend indeed.
2. He who laughs last laughs best.
3. Youth means limitless possibilities.
4. Strike while the iron is hot.
5. You mustn't play football in the classroom.
6. Man struggles upwards; water flows downwards.
7. Nowadays, studying English gains popularity in China.
8. An apple a day keeps the doctor away.

Task 2

> Memo
>
> To: All students
> From: Chen Tao
> Date: August 20, 2011
> Subject: Discussion on the Class Discipline
>
> All the students should have the class meeting at 7 p.m. on August 22, 2011 to discuss the class discipline. No one should be absent. Anyone who can not be present should call Mr. Guo in advance. If there is any question, please consult Chen Tao.

Script for Listening Comprehension

Part I Listening Comprehension

Task 1

Directions: *In this section you will hear 10 sentences. You are required to circle the word that you hear in brackets.*

1. We saw the (cup/<u>cop</u>).

答案及听力材料

2. Better (<u>wit</u>/wet) than wealth.

3. (Ears/<u>Years</u>) bring wisdom.

4. Merry (<u>meet</u>/met), merry part.

5. (<u>Learn</u>/Lean) to walk before you can run.

6. A tree is known by (<u>its</u>/eats) fruit.

7. Doing is better than (<u>saying</u>/seeing).

8. He (through/<u>threw</u>) the ball up and caught it again.

9. There are a thousand and (won/<u>one</u>) stars in the sky.

10. It's all (<u>right</u>/write) to borrow money occasionally, but don't let it become a habit.

Task 2

Directions: *In this section you will hear one word from each of the following groups of words. Circle the one you hear.*

1. word   2. unit   3. beam   4. fine   5. down   6. boats
7. roads   8. lord   9. mouse   10. slow

Task 3

Directions: *This section is to test your ability to give proper responses. There are 5 recorded questions in it. After each question, there is a pause. When you hear a question, you should decide on the correct answer from the 4 choices marked A, B, C and D.*

1. Is this pen yours?

2. Who's on duty today?

3. How about going fishing tomorrow?

4. What do you do for a living?

5. What are you going to do next weekend?

Task 4

Directions: *This section is to test your ability to understand short dialogues. There are 5 recorded dialogues in it. After each dialogue, there is a recorded question. When you hear a question, you should decide on the correct answer from the 4 choices marked A, B, C and D.*

1. W: I read an article by a girl from England.

M: Really? Tell me more about her.

　　Q: What are they talking about?

2. W: We can not travel by underground to the Summer Palace.

　　M: But we can take a bus. It takes more than an hour.

　　Q: What's the man tell the woman?

3. M: Monika, have you got everything ready for the board meeting this morning?

　　W: Yes, Mr. Rogers. The meeting begins in Room 504 at 9 o'clock.

　　Q: Where is the meeting held?

4. M: Morning, madam. What's the trouble with you?

　　M: I seem to have a fever, and feel a headache.

　　Q: Where are they?

5. M: What kind of food do you like in particular?

　　W: I'm particularly fond of sour cream

　　Q: Which food does the woman like?

Task 5

Directions: *In this section, you will hear a short passage. There are five missing words or phrases in it. Fill in the blanks with the exact words or phrases you hear.*

Shopping for clothes is not the same <u>experience</u> for a man as it is for a woman. A man goes shopping because he needs something. He knows what he wants. His object is to find it and <u>buy</u> it, but the price isn't the first consideration. Next let's see a woman shops in the opposite way. Her shopping is not often <u>based</u> on need. She usually hasn't made up her mind what she wants, so she is only "having a look around". Faced with a roomful of dresses, a woman can <u>spend</u> an hour easily going from one rack to another, while few men have the same <u>patience</u>.

Key to Unit 6

Part I　Listening Comprehension

Task 1

　　1. wash　2. share　3. fetched　4. words　5. feather　6. room　7. cocks

答案及听力材料

8. sells   9. bowl   10. girl

Task 2

1. leak   2. gap   3. soup   4. up   5. floor   6. cede

7. hurt   8. map   9. let   10. head

Task 3

1. D   2. B   3. D   4. D   5. B

Task 4

1. D   2. C   3. C   4. C   5. B

Task 5

1. warm   2. green   3. comfortable   4. harvest   5. gathered

Part Ⅱ   Dialogue

Task 1

1. E   2. F   3. C   4. B   5. A

Task 2

1. E   2. A   3. F   4. C   5. B   6. D   7. G   8. J   9. H   10. I

Part Ⅲ   Vocabulary & Structure

Task 1

1. D   2. D   3. C   4. C   5. A   6. A   7. D   8. C   9. D

10. B   11. B   12. A   13. A   14. C   15. D

Task 2

1. appearance   2. entertainment   3. donation   4. emergency   5. express

6. differently   7. allowed   8. actual   9. education   10. Honesty

Task 3

a. decision; decisive; decide

b. consideration; considering; considerate

c. agreed; agreement; disagreed

d. emergency; emerged; emergence

e. diplomat; Diplomacy; diplomatic

119

Task 4

1. He passed through a difficult period shortly after his marriage broke down.
2. He has blossomed into a man.
3. He blurt out the truth.
4. You should know how to deal with this problem.
5. The TV programme is not up to par tonight.
6. We want to raise our children to be outstanding talent.
7. When you meet something in trouble, firstly you must cool down.
8. She looks young, but she's actually 50.

Part Ⅳ Reading Comprehension

Task 1

1. A 2. B 3. C 4. C 5. B

Task 2

1. B A 2. I K 3. O N 4. P Q 5. E H

Task 3

1. John Smith 2. Asian Economic studies 3. December 22nd, 2011
4. about one hundred 5. Economic Development

Task 4

1. Scotland 2. the Romans 3. hard 4. a thistle 5. wiped out

Part Ⅴ Translation

1. A 2. A 3. A 4. B 5. A 6. C

Part Ⅵ Writing

Task 1

1. Out of sight, out of mind.
2. My best friend is different from my other friends.
3. Time is so precious that we can't afford to waste it.
4. Rome was not built in a day.
5. We should get into the habit of keeping good hours.

答案及听力材料

6. I had the meanest mother in the whole world.
7. It is conceivable that knowledge plays an important role in our life.
8. Mother said she was glad she never let her hair be cut.

Task 2

> June 19, 2011
>
> Dear Mr. John Brown,
>
>   Thank you for your ordering our latest products. The goods you've ordered have delivered and they will arrive in about a week. Please write back to confirm it when you have received the goods. We look forward to further cooperation with you.
>
>   Yours sincerely,
>   Wang Ming
>   Sales Manager

Script for Listening Comprehension

Part Ⅰ Listening Comprehension

Task 1

Directions: *In this section you will hear 10 sentences. You are required to circle the word that you hear in brackets.*

1. Who is going to (<u>wash</u>/wish) it?
2. Would you like to (spare/<u>share</u>) it?
3. He (<u>fetched</u>/fished) it for me.
4. Do you know all the (<u>words</u>/worlds)?
5. Birds of a (<u>feather</u>/father) flock together.
6. You would better stay in the (zoo/<u>room</u>) for a day or two.
7. There are three (<u>cocks</u>/corks) over there.
8. Mary (shells/<u>sells</u>) peas.
9. I saw a red (bull/<u>bowl</u>).

10. That was a very good (goal/<u>girl</u>).

Task 2

Directions: *In this section you will hear one word from each of the following groups of words. Circle the one you hear.*

1. leak   2. gap   3. soup   4. up   5. floor   6. cede

7. hurt   8. map   9. let   10. head

Task 3

Directions: *This section is to test your ability to give proper responses. There are 5 recorded questions in it. After each question, there is a pause. When you hear a question, you should decide on the correct answer from the 4 choices marked A, B, C and D.*

1. What's the weather like today?

2. It's a fine day today. What are you going to do?

3. Can you tell me where I can park my car?

4. Is this your first trip to London?

5. Excuse me, may I see your boss?

Task 4

Directions: *This section is to test your ability to understand short dialogues. There are 5 recorded dialogues in it. After each dialogue, there is a recorded question. When you hear a question, you should decide on the correct answer from the 4 choices marked A, B, C and D.*

1. W: Did you go to the job fair yesterday?

   M: Yes. It was really too crowded there.

   Q: Where did the woman go?

2. W: Wei Bin is an honest man.

   M: Yes, he is friendly and helpful

   Q: What does the man think of Wei Bin?

3. M: How many people took part in the conference?

   W: We had expected 40 people, but only 25 people turned up.

   Q: How many people were absent from the conference?

4. W: The traffic was so bad this morning.

M: Yes, it's. As it was really snowy. It took me longer to the station.

Q: What's the weather like?

5. M: Shall we have the meeting at ten o'clock on Wednesday morning?

W: Wednesday morning at ten? It's OK for me.

Q: What are they talking about?

Task 5

Directions*: In this section, you will hear a short passage. There are five missing words or phrases in it. Fill in the blanks with the exact words or phrases you hear.*

There are four seasons in a year. They are spring, summer, autumn and winter. I like spring and autumn. The weather becomes <u>warm</u> gradually in spring. We can see flowers and hear the songs of the birds. The forests and the woods seem to be awakened and covered with <u>green</u> color. In autumn the sky is blue and we feel <u>comfortable</u>. The autumn is the <u>harvest</u> time. The fruits are picked and the crops are <u>gathered</u> in. We can eat fresh apples, bananas, peaches, oranges and grapes.